PRAISE FOR
OPEN SOURCE CHURCH

"God calls us together because of who God is. God is not a dry, detached singular being, but a holy community. We are made in God's image. So we are designed to be together. The church needs to hear, believe, and live this reality in every facet of its life. Together we are smarter, better, even more faithful, than any one of us can possibly be individually. Any attempt to limit the openness, the variety and innovation of the whole in the name of the few (or the one) inevitably undercuts the life of faith. In part, this is the message of Landon Whitsitt's *Open Source Church*. But there's much more here. What we need today is churchly thinking for 'what's next.' And, as Landon knows, 'what's next' will certainly not be a single model of church. Of course, there has never been just one single way of being the church any way – never! In this book, Landon provides a vivid and compelling picture of 'what's next.' Welcome to the future!"

—*Michael Jinkins, president and professor of theology, Louisville Presbyterian Theological Seminary and author of Louisville Seminary's* Thinking Out Loud *blog*

"Whitsett offers a model for changing church structures that could work. He translates the principles of open source technology to imagine a new framework for fluid and faithful mission. If you are searching for more responsive, agile, and inclusive-of-all-generations ways to organize church life, read this book."

—*Melissa Wiginton, Vice President for Education Beyond the Walls, Austin Presbyterian Theological Seminary*

"Whitsitt envisions a church where openness and inclusion don't just affect what happens at the front door but become the cornerstone upon which the entire structure is built."

— *Eric Elnes, Host,* Darkwood Brew *and author of* The Phoenix Affirmations

"Landon Whitsitt's vision of a new kind of church is revolutionary and hopeful, particularly for faithful men and women who feel they are locked into systems that are shutting down with very few reasons to hope for a reboot. What Chris Anderson's book *Free* did for the tech and business sectors, Landon Whitsitt's *Open Source Church* looks poised to do for the Church —open up access points to new ways of thinking about how we function and who we are. This is not a book about churches embracing new media and new technology. This is a book about our churches installing a whole new, participatory operating system. The innovation we need for forming faith communities in this new era of mission will come from this kind of thinking."

—*Steve Knight, community architect for TransFORM Network (www.transformnetwork.org) and team member for the Hope Partnership for Missional Transformation (part of the Christian Church/Disciples of Christ)*

Open Source Church is the most effective metaphor I've read in years for expressing the kinds of community that Jesus' followers are called to create and to live. For Christians under 40 or so, and for more seekers than you can imagine, the open-source world is everyday reality. People today connect through facebook and google, through social media and peer-to-peer networking. If the church is to be a vibrant social force in our day, it can only be an open source church.

— *Philip Clayton, author of* Transforming Christian Theology

Open Source Church

OPEN SOURCE CHURCH

Making Room for the Wisdom of All

~

Landon Whitsitt

 | ALBAN

Herndon, Virginia
www.alban.org

The Alban Institute
2121 Cooperative Way, Suite 100
Herndon, VA 20171

Unless otherwise noted, all Scripture quotations are from the New Revised Standard Version of the Bible, © 1989, Division of Christian Education of the National Council of Churches of Christ in the United States of America, and are used by permission.

Cover design by Signal Hill.

Library of Congress Cataloging-in-Publication Data

Whitsitt, Landon, 1976-
  Open source church : making room for the wisdom of all / Landon Whitsitt.
      p. cm.
  Includes bibliographical references.
  ISBN 978-1-56699-412-5
  1. Church renewal. I. Title.
  BV600.3.W533 2011
  262.001'7--dc22
                              2011004788

11   12   13   14   15   V G   5   4   3   2   1

~ Contents ~

123797

Foreword

I stood in the kitchen, knowing that I needed to end the phone conversation, but it was hard. I wanted to stay connected with my friend on the other end of the line. I was at the University of Nebraska, taking some art courses, and my friend was at the University of Michigan. We had lost contact since we moved far away from each other. He said, "Just email me." Then he gave me a strange address, being sure to specify that it included "the at sign—the one looks like an 'a' inside a circle." He further explained to me that I shouldn't use any spaces or it wouldn't work.

"Um. Okay," I answered, and after shifting my eyes side to side uncomfortably, I scribbled down the meaningless string of letters and symbols.

"It's easy," he assured me. "Just set up an account."

It was the first email address I had ever received and it was a few months later before I got dial-up Internet access and set up my first Hotmail account. I figured that I would use email to jot down a couple of lines to a few of my close friends, who were really into computers. I didn't realize how much my life would change with that small step.

There is a lot of mystery involved in a simple email. When I write a letter, I have a pretty good idea of how that works. I get out a piece of paper, write words on that paper, and put it in an envelope. I carefully inscribe the address on the envelope, affix a sign of my payment on the letter, and mail it. Then a series of people and vehicles make sure that the letter gets to the destination. If I spell a name wrong or make a noncrucial error in the address, often the mail carrier can still get the letter to the correct house or office.

Yet, I can't really tell you what's happening when I send mail electronically. I understand that I need Internet access and an email address. I can tell you that I can't make any spelling errors in the address. I know the process involved on my end. From then on, it's a mystery. There are email clients, browsers, servers and networks. I've even been told that the procedure has to do with a series of ones and zeros. When I hear that, something in my brain clicks off, things become foggy, and I don't really understand anything else.

Even though I can't fully comprehend how email works, I do understand that it has drastically changed my life and ministry. Since those days in college, I went to seminary, and became a pastor. Now, as a minister in an urban congregation, I spend most of my office hours reading, answering, and generating emails. I cannot quite leave work at the office, because I carry around a virtual inbox in my pocket, located on my iPhone. I can wake up in the middle of the night, with something burning on my mind, and write an email to someone in our church. Most people in our congregation expect an email reply within 24 hours. I have stopped using "Dear" and "Sincerely" in my correspondence. I have to be careful not to forget "please" and "thank you." My communication does not carry a particular feel or smell. And I have to remember that some people sound much more abrupt on email than they do face-to-face.

Email has changed the way that I do pastoral care. I receive private messages—communication that is written when it's dark outside, and when people are living through a dark night of the soul. Though I treat these messages as confidential, I must remember that my emails can be easily forwarded or distributed to a large number of people with the press of a few buttons. My emails are not private correspondence.

In a relatively short time, email has become my primary means of communication. In fact, sometimes it's hard to remember how I pastored without it. I don't understand exactly how it works, but it has become central to the way that I communicate, operate, manage, and think.

Technology often affects our lives that way. As Marshall McLuhan noted, technology is an extension of the human body. As my car is an extension of the foot, email has become an extension of my mouth. We begin to use technology mindlessly, and then it begins to change our minds. It affects basic things in our lives, like the way that we organize and lead.

Just as email changed the way we minister and carry out our business, we're also surrounded by the generative, creative outcomes of open source models. We may not fully understand how much our lives are affected by them. We might use Wikipedia as a resource or Firefox as our web browser, without any thought about the process of how they came (and are coming) into being. Yet, the open source methodology, the practice that encourages the wisdom of the crowds, is quickly changing how we function.

That's why, as church leaders, it's important to have practical theologians who can and will engage the ways in which our technology informs and forms our thought. And that is why *Open Source Church* is so important. Even if this is the first time you have thought about the term "open source," Landon

Whitsitt's poignant analysis helps us to understand the crucial shifts that are occurring all around us and how they impact our congregations.

But that's not the only reason this book is vital. Landon's insight as a full-time pastor and a swivel-chair techie will fearlessly guide us in how open source methodology is changing how we organize and lead; in addition, it will help us to make nimble connections to our best church traditions and scriptural insight so that we can imagine where we ought to be. The Open Source Church is a metaphor rich with possibilities. It will spark your congregation's creativity, give you a new vocabulary, and renew your prophetic imagination. As we begin to practice the sort of de-centering, Christ-filled, participatory leadership that Landon describes, we will reshape the way that we do church. When we can live into open source ideals, we can gain a fresh understanding of the good news of Jesus Christ.

Carol Howard Merritt
Pastor, Western Presbyterian Church

Preface

1. I love the church. "Church Geek" is a label I wear proudly. I love church meetings. I love worship. I love Bible study. I love church, and I have been exposed to many different forms of it.

When I was younger, my family attended charismatic evangelical churches (yes, we were Holy Rollers), then Vineyard churches, then a Southern Baptist church. I went to college at a Presbyterian college and liked to say that I was "Presbyterian by default." Then I met a nice girl and became "Presbyterian by Marriage," and, after we had our first child, I joined a Presbyterian church and became "A Born-Again Presbyterian." I have extensively worked and worshiped with Roman Catholics, Anglicans, all kinds of Methodists, and Disciples of Christ. I even toyed with joining each of those denominations at various times. I like to say that I am a one-man ecumenical movement, and throughout it all was this marvelous thing called "The Church."

In every age, God has gathered women and men together to join in the divine work of bringing healing and reconciliation

to the world. In every time and place, God's Holy Spirit has
animated a group of gathered people charged with spreading
Christ's grace and peace to the world. In all times and in all
places, God has called the church into being as the very real,
present body of Christ for the world.

The church is a beautiful thing.

2. I am, by nature, not one to simply take what has been
handed me as the gospel truth. But I wouldn't go so
far as to say that I'm a contrarian. I would rather say
that I like the possibility and potential of things far more than
their present reality. If I can't poke it, prod it, question it, poke
holes in it, edit it, amend it, or revise it, then I usually don't
find much value in something. Even if that something is a way
of doing church.

By the time I arrived in Louisville, Kentucky, on July 4, 2002,
to attend Louisville Presbyterian Theological Seminary, I had
already been thinking about the church and what it was destined
to be and become. I had gone to seminary on the faith that the
church God was calling me to serve was not the church of my
parents' and grandparents' years, but a new church. All of my
lessons confirmed this. The people of God, we were taught, were
always being called to proclaim the gospel in new and different
ways, depending on their context. In fact, I decided that, for the
church to be faithful, it had to be willing to change.

And that meant poking and prodding and questioning. It
meant reforming and being reformed. It meant a future that is
faithful to the past.

3. I often like to say that classes at Louisville Seminary
were not the only source of my theological education.
I believe that a significant reason God called my family to Louisville was to meet and become a part of Covenant

Community Church. CCC was the church that I had mapped out in my notebooks during those long months before moving from Lawrence, Kansas, to Louisville. Right before my eyes, I was witnessing a working model of what I already thought the church should look like. Right before my eyes was a group of God-gathered people poking and prodding, questioning and revising what church could look like. Here, I had found another source of my education.

For the next four years my family lived and breathed this new vision of the church. We learned about God's call to mission and of how we are each responsible for ensuring that ministry is done in the world. We learned that if Christ's grace and peace was going to be spread it had to be us to do it, because, while the leadership constantly tried to equip us to be Christ's hands and feet, they were not going to deny us the opportunity to get messy. It was at CCC that we learned that God is calling *all people to mission and ministry, not just a few.*

4. The people who have influenced my thinking about an open source church and writing a book are too numerous to name. Like any good open source project, many people have simply given the material a test drive to see how it works, while others have dived into the nuts and bolts of the project and radically shifted my thinking on various points. I hesitate to name any one person, so let me say, from the bottom of my heart, that I feel indebted to each and every one of you.

But there are a few I must name.

Thank you, Barclay, Dustin, Ryan, and Neal, for keeping me full of coffee.

Thank you, Beth. You made this book better.

Thank you, First Presbyterian Church, for exploring these crazy ideas with me.

Thank you, Jud and Liz, for being my first models of a new kind of pastor. I still mimic you both daily.

Thank you, Twitterverse, for engaging in this conversation with me every day.

Thank you, Scott, Scotty, Brett, and Deacon. Many of these arguments began during study break.

Thank you, COTE, for asking many of these questions for me.

Thank you, Dr. Ray, for teaching me to think theologically.

Thank you, Jamie. You are my theological brother.

Thank you, Will. You are the pastoral leader I always try to live up to.

Thank you, Jacob, for giving me an opportunity to explain this idea.

Thank you, Jayne and Bill, for showing me what living the call of God looks like.

Thank you, Bruce, for letting me walk with you as you talked "new church" on the national level. #pants

Thank you, Rocky, for the years of conversation we have shared. Our early stabs (in "the notebook") on the role and function of a pastor were formative for me.

Thank you, Brian, for sparring with me on Sunday nights as we reflected on the previous week's work as pastors. You have kept me honest to the call of ministry.

Thank you, Chad, for helping me realize that I had something to say and encouraging me to say it. I wouldn't have done this without your prodding.

Thank you, Carol, for all the guidance and encouragement, for all the edits and all the commiseration. You're a good partner to have.

Thank you, Lady, for helping me find the space and courage to write so I could fulfill a dream.

~ Chapter One ~

The Open Source Church

I f I said the words *open source*, many people would have no idea what I was talking about. If they did, they would most likely think about software, such as the Firefox Web browser or the Linux operating system.

When I tell many people I am writing a book on open source church, they look at me funny, wondering, What do you mean by *open source church*? Therefore, if I am going to talk with others about an open source church and be understood, I need to begin by explaining what open source is.

Open source, when referring to software particularly, simply means that the basic instructions for a program are open for anyone to see and edit. This is in contrast to closed source software, which is closed off to everyone except a privileged few.

Like software, churches can also be open or closed. Many of us have experienced a closed church. These are the churches where a select few people seem to run the show. Often nothing gets done without their approval, but occasionally it is merely their input that is solicited, input that carries significant weight in the decision-making process. An *open source church*, however, is one in which the basic functions of mission and ministry are open to anyone. Members feel free to pursue their callings from God without being forced to jump through hoops in order to do so. They do not need to sit through multiple committee meetings for approval, and they run the risk of being told no only if what they propose to do violates a common, basic understanding of what God has called the church to be and do.

But why is the idea of open source and the open source movement itself important? Why should anyone care?

The best story I know of to illustrate the need for and the importance of the open source idea is about a man who some say is the godfather of the open source movement, Richard Stallman. Stallman was a computer programmer at Massachusetts Institute of Technology as well as the founder of the Free Software Foundation. While working at MIT, Stallman wanted to modify the code of a printer that repeatedly jammed. The printer the department members shared was on another floor, so going to retrieve a document only to find that the printer had jammed threw his (and everyone else's) workload behind. The printer had been a gift from the Xerox Corporation. It was their cutting-edge model and not a gift you turned down. But it kept jamming.

Stallman had addressed the same issue on the department's previous printer by modifying the software to notify a user when her print job was complete and by notifying all users when the machine was jammed. It had worked brilliantly, and he wanted to do the same thing to the new printer. Xerox, however, would not provide Stallman with the source code for the printer's program. The printer's license agreement defined the code as private information (proprietary or closed), and Xerox would not release it.

At its most basic level, the open source software movement is about making sure that things can work for everyone. If people like Richard Stallman do not receive the access necessary to make software better, software might never be better than it is today.

If Christians let it, this value of making sure that things can work for everyone can have an effect on our churches as well. There is an old joke that makes its way around churches every so often: Someone, usually a pastor, stands up in the pulpit for the Sunday morning service and says, "Do you all know what the seven last words of the church are?" The congregation looks at her or him dumbfounded. No one knows what these words are. The old preacher smiles slyly and says, "We've never done it that way before."

Every church has a set of rules. Usually the rules are unwritten. As author, blogger, and pastor Carol Howard Merritt says in her book *Tribal Church,* these "invisible rulebooks" have usually developed over years and years and years of making mistakes, correcting them, and ensuring that the congregation never makes those mistakes again. When someone new comes into our churches, they don't know about our rulebooks. They don't know that you can't put this table there or open that door or put up that sign. When new members try to make church "work better," they often feel like Richard Stallman being told by Xerox that he could not have access to the source code of the printer. They want to be able to participate in even the smallest activities of the church (setting up the tables in the fellowship hall), but the select few who seem to be guarding these unwritten rules consistently shut down their efforts.

Being an open source church is about making sure people can do the things they think they need to do to make church work for them. Too often churches and their organizational structures are so firmly established that it is virtually impossible for someone to come to the church and begin contributing to its life in a meaningful way. These new people feel like they are stuck at every turn.

Although the established members don't mean to shut a new person down (in fact, they think they are doing all they can to initiate the new member into "the way we do business"), it doesn't take long for new members to conclude that their contributions are not wanted, needed, or valued. What would you do if every time you suggested a new idea, you were told that the church had either already tried that or that it wouldn't work here or that we are not the kind of church that would do something like that? I can tell you what I would do. I would go find another church.

Most people want to have a church experience that is more open than it is closed. They want to be a part of a group that will accept their contributions, not force them to merely be a cog in another machine. By and large, being treated like a cog is what people deal with every day at their jobs. People don't get to be creative. They are implicitly (and sometimes explicitly) told that their purpose in that organization is simply to fulfill their job description. The organization makes clear to them that they are a part of something larger than themselves, and all they need to accomplish is the task set before them so that someone else can accomplish another task. Many organizations function like an assembly line, where those performing each job along the way are replaceable. Very rarely does a person find a job that explicitly states they are supposed to come up with new ideas or be creative.

Why can't the church be the one place in someone's life where it is not only acceptable but also expected that they act creatively and contribute significantly to the life of the church community and the community at large? If we Christians understand God to be the "creator of heaven and earth," and if we believe that we are all made in God's image, then why can't the church be the place where we each find permission to operate out of that understanding and belief?

I believe this is precisely the kind of place the church should be.

Free as in Beer and Free as in Speech

Ultimately, the open source movement is a discussion about what freedom is and how all of us use that freedom. Pertinent questions are: Who decides what freedom is? Is there a limit to the amount of freedom any person or group should have? Does the freedom of one person or group mean that another person or group doesn't have freedom? If everyone is exercising a lot of freedom, how do we tell someone or some group that they can't do whatever it is they are doing?

A popular way of talking about freedom in the open source movement is to differentiate between the terms *gratis* and *libre*. The word *gratis* means that a piece of software does not cost anything to obtain or use. This is not to say the software doesn't have value (it very much does), only that someone will not be required to offer anything of value in exchange for that piece of software. You don't have to pay money to obtain or use it. Such software is often called *freeware* and is referred to as being "free as in beer."

On the other hand, when people in the open source software movement say that something is *libre*, they are referring to the fact that the piece of software has no restrictions placed upon it. If software is libre, you cannot dictate who uses the software, the reasons for its use, or whether or not it can be modified. Those of us who are residents of the United States of America are taught this understanding of the word *freedom* with our first lesson in civics. We are taught that in our country we are "free" to be and do and pursue whatever it is that we want to be, do, and pursue. When we say that we have "freedom," we mean that no restrictions are placed upon us as long as we behave in a manner that does not restrict anyone else. It is in this regard that we would say something is "free as in speech."

These ideas—free as in beer and free as in speech—are important to the open source movement. However, it is not only the open source movement that can claim them. One could say that that these twin ideas are an integral part of the way we understand what is required of us as Christians. Together, gratis and libre form the basis of Christian ethics, an idea thoroughly explored in a short piece by Martin Luther.

Luther struggled to help his contemporaries understand what it means to be a Christian in relation to others. In the tract "The Freedom of a Christian," Luther explains the basis of Christian ethics by exploring two propositions:

A Christian is a perfectly free Lord of all, subject to none.
A Christian is a perfectly dutiful servant of all, subject to all.

With the first proposition, Luther says that because Christians are joined to Christ in faith, God has forgiven our sins and requires nothing more of us in a *spiritual* sense. We are forgiven, we are one with God, and we are free to live without the fear of damnation. This forgiveness means that we are free of the obligation to earn favor with God through good works (one of his chief complaints about the Roman Catholic Church of his time).

Luther famously spent hours, months, years trying to please God. Luther had been taught that he owed God something, and so he spent much of his life trying to figure out how to repay God whatever it was that he owed. Luther spent hours in prayer and in reading the Bible. He participated in the sacraments. But he was never convinced that those actions had any lasting effects on the state of his soul.

In reading the book of Romans Luther discovered that his salvation did not depend upon anything he might do; rather, it depended upon what God had already done for him. Luther began to understand that his faith in God was in fact a gift from God. He began to understand that he could do nothing on his own to earn God's forgiveness and be acceptable in God's sight. Luther began to preach that God's gift of grace and peace is freely given to us. It is always already ours. Because of the work and person of Jesus Christ, Luther said, a Christian is free, having received the benefits of the perfect life and sacrifice of Jesus Christ.

But Luther also wanted to make clear that we have work to do. In Luther's understanding, we are people with two natures, one "spiritual" and one "bodily." Even though we are already justified before God because of the work and person of Jesus Christ, we must still contend with the reality that we behave according to impulses not of God. As Luther famously said, "We are at the same time justified and sinners." Luther believed that when we recognize that we were always already forgiven by God, we develop a desire to serve God with our whole being. And to accomplish this, or as Luther says, "bring our bodies into subjection," we do good works as a way of conditioning our bodily nature to act in a way that demonstrates love of God. And so we do those good works, recognizing that they do nothing to save us or make us more acceptable in God's sight. Rather, we do good works for others in order to imitate the way God has treated us through Christ, thereby ensuring that our entire selves are loving and praising God. That is why as Christians, Luther says, we are "subject to all."

Following from Luther, the open source ideas of gratis and libre are woven into Christians' very DNA. In one sense, Christians are libre. We are bound by nothing. Nothing is required of us. Because God has given us our faith, faith that allows us to receive the grace of Christ, we stand before creation unencumbered. Yet, in another sense, Christians are gratis. We understand ourselves to be *not our own*. Even though we stand before God completely justified, we still need to bring every piece of our self into alignment with Christ, the one who, as Paul wrote to the Philippians, "did not regard equality with God as something to be exploited, but emptied himself, taking the form of a slave, being born in human likeness. And being found in human form, he humbled himself and became obedient to the point of death—even death on a cross" (Phil. 2:6–8). The works we do should mirror the works Christ does. Being like Christ means that we give ourselves away and expect nothing in return. It's not that our works have no value, only that we expect no payment for our works. We do our works to benefit others and as a way of training ourselves to be like Christ.

An Open Source Definition

One of the early problems of the open source software movement was that, while everyone agreed that freedom and openness are good things, there was little consistency about how much or what kind of freedom and openness we were talking about. Some people wanted to emphasize the gratis side of freedom and said software should not cost anything. Others wanted to emphasize the libre side of freedom and openness and believed that once someone paid for a piece of software, they were free to do with it whatever they wished.

Many different software licenses were developed in attempts to define what is and is not open source. As the open source movement began to grow and gain speed, there arose a need for some definitive criteria that would enable the community to say "This is open software" and "This is not." Into that void stepped Bruce Perens and "the Open Source Definition (OSD)." Perens himself notes that the OSD is not a software license but "a specification of what is permissible in a software license for that software to be referred to as open source."[1] Since its publication in February 1998, the OSD has been the go-to document as the movement has grown and changed.

What is truly remarkable about Perens's work is that he managed, in one document, to accommodate the twin ideas of gratis and libre. Not only does the OSD speak to how a piece of software is obtained but it also addresses what rights the owner has in regard to that piece of software. The OSD has ten criteria that must be met if a piece of software is going to be labeled open source. I like to refer to the OSD as "The Ten Commandments of Open Source." As I am sure you will see, the criteria not only provide the open source software movement with a consistent and unifying voice but also offer other open source ideologies (such as open source Christianity) with a foundation on which to build and explore.

Let's take a look at the ten criteria of the OSD in order to gain a basic understanding of what it means to view software as open source. At the same time, I will reframe the ten criteria as religious principles or ideas to help us begin thinking about Christianity as an open source reality. This is important because I want us to understand that constructing an open source model of church leadership, structure, and organization is not simply a fun trick, nor is it an idea that has no underlying, intentional guiding philosophy. To say that a church is an open source church is to say that, at its heart, a church views the world in a particular way and then tries to organize and structure itself according to that worldview. The open source model of church leadership, structure, and organization I will present in the later chapters of this book can be tied to a worldview consistent with a Christian reframing of the ten criteria of the OSD.

Criterion 1: Free Redistribution

The first criterion listed in the OSD is free redistribution. If a piece of software is going to be considered open source, not only may anyone make as many copies of the software as they want but they may also sell or give them away without paying for the privilege of doing so. The rationale given in the annotated edition of the OSD is that this criterion eliminates the temptation for those associated with the software to abandon long-term gain for short-term sales.[2]

In similar fashion, the gospel has been freely received by us all and is likewise to be given freely and without requirement. The question that this idea raises for me is, what is the gospel? If we are going to say that something is received and given, what exactly is that thing? Even though the correlation between the open source software movement and an exploration of an open source Christian worldview is not one to one, thinking about the gospel as I would a piece of software or a computer program is helpful to me.

If you want to listen to music on your computer, what do you do? Most of you start some music playing program (iTunes, Windows Media Player, Songbird, Rhythmbox, and the like). If you want to write a letter, you open a word processing program (Microsoft Word, OpenOffice Writer, for example). When you want to send and receive e-mail, you open your e-mail client (Outlook, Thunderbird, and others). All of these programs were built to help you accomplish certain goals, to make your life easier and better (in some cases). I think of *the gospel* as roughly equivalent to software and computer programs in that it exists to accomplish a certain goal: to ensure our freedom. Whether we are bound to outmoded ways of thinking or self-destructive behaviors, held captive emotionally or physically, or crippled by personal struggle or systemic injustice, the gospel of Jesus Christ exists to set us free.

I believe that as the people of God, we have an opportunity to proclaim a timeless truth: *To proclaim Jesus Christ is to proclaim freedom, and to proclaim freedom is to proclaim Jesus Christ.*

When I look at that sentence, I cannot think of anything I believe that is more true or more biblical. The unfortunate reality, however, is that much of life (especially the church) is guided not by freedom but by a need to control—a need for power. The church in many places has changed from an institution that teaches postures, approaches, and behaviors that lead to freedom to an institution that teaches postures, approaches,

and behaviors that will maintain itself. A gracious way of saying it is that the church intends to teach us effective ways of
organizing ourselves or beneficial ways of believing that lead
to freedom, but opportunities for graciousness are becoming
fewer and farther between. Churches have developed structural
habits that many in leadership are loath to abandon, for those
habits have proven effective in ensuring the continuation of
the organization, and "leading" these organizations results in
personal acclaim for many.

But the gospel is not concerned with maintaining structures
or preserving doctrine. The gospel is concerned with freedom.
The gospel begins and ends with the life, death, and resurrection
of Jesus Christ. If there is no Jesus Christ, there is no gospel.[3] As
Christians, we claim that in Jesus Christ, God has been revealed.
If we want to know the intention of God, we look to the intention of Jesus. In Luke 4:18–19, he states his intention clearly:
"The Spirit of the Lord is upon me, because he has anointed
me to bring good news to the poor. He has sent me to proclaim
release to the captives and recovery of sight to the blind, to let
the oppressed go free, to proclaim the year of the Lord's favor."
In John 10:10, Jesus states his intention in another way: "The
thief comes only to steal and kill and destroy. I came that they
may have life, and have it abundantly."

Repeatedly throughout the biblical texts we find Jesus re-
storing, healing, and raising. He dramatically teaches against
captivity of any kind—physical, mental, emotional, spiritual.
Jesus identifies with those who are suffering. He seeks to enter
their reality and set them free from their bondage. Once free,
he commands them to go and live a life of freedom.

The life of freedom that Jesus proclaims (which he calls *the
kingdom of God*) is an affront to those in power, and it ultimately leads to his death. Yet even though he was put to death,
through his resurrection he unleashed the power of freedom for
all creation. The new life of Christ ensures that no boundary

can hold us captive, no shackles can keep us oppressed. In Christ's death and resurrection, freedom has overcome captivity and oppression.

So, if we think of this gospel as roughly equivalent to a computer program, and under the first criterion of the OSD a computer program is freely redistributable, then what does it mean to say that the gospel is also freely redistributable?

This criterion draws heavily on the idea of freedom as gratis. No one is required to pay for the privilege of using a piece of software. (Nothing would stop me from selling my copy to you, but the fact that you also could obtain your own copy of the software free of charge would make my reselling scheme fall flat on its face.) When we apply this idea to the gospel, we are claiming that there is nothing you must give in exchange for this thing whose purpose is to set you free. We do not have to "pay" for our freedom.

For instance, some Christians claim that if you don't pay for the gospel by asking Jesus to come into your heart, then you are not entitled to the freedom promised in the gospel. Other Christian groups suggest that unless you pay for the gospel by joining their particular church, you will not receive the freedom promised in the gospel.

But when an open source Christianity abides by its first commandment, "Thou shalt freely give what thou hast freely received," our lives begin to reflect the truth that God has freely given *all* people the gospel so that we might *all* live an abundant life. To steal the words of the *Godly Play* curriculum, the gospel is "like a present." And like any present, "you don't have to take them, or buy them, or get them in any way. They already belong to you."[4]

Criterion 2: Access to Source Code

The second criterion given in the OSD regards a software's source code. In the software world, the term *source code* refers

to computer instructions written in a form that human beings
can understand. For example, here is a snippet of a source code
written in the Java programming language:[5]

```
/**
 * A partial implementation of a hypo-
thetical stock portfolio class.
 * We use it only to demonstrate number
and date internationalization.
 */
public class Portfolio {
EquityPosition[] positions;
Date lastQuoteTime = new Date();
public void print() {
// Obtain NumberFormat and DateFormat
objects to format our data.
NumberFormat number = NumberFormat.get-
Instance();
NumberFormat price = NumberFormat.get-
CurrencyInstance();
NumberFormat percent = NumberFormat.get-
PercentInstance();
DateFormat shortdate = DateFormat.
getDateInstance(DateFormat.SHORT);
DateFormat fulldate = DateFormat.
getDateTimeInstance(DateFormat.LONG,
DateFormat.LONG);
```

You will notice words you recognize in the text; we are not
dealing with zeros and ones here. The words of the source code
taken together add up to specific instructions that you may or
may not understand, even if you do know what the words *date*
and *format* mean.

To be considered an open source program, the program's
source code must be made available by the developer in the

software package itself or as a download. Part of the intention behind the open source software movement is to allow programs to be modified to meet the needs of those people using them. If people do not have access to the source code, they cannot perform any repairs or modifications. Access to source code is fundamental to the success of a particular piece of software and to the open source movement in general. Access to source code is also fundamental to the "success" of the gospel, but what is the gospel's source code?

Christians have claimed that Jesus Christ is the revelation of God—the Word of God made flesh (John 1:14). We claim that Jesus Christ is God in human form—that God chose to become like us and live with us in order to have a relationship with us and lead us to freedom. We point to the first chapter of the Gospel of John, and the idea of Logos found there, as our starting point for understanding Jesus Christ as this incarnate Word of God—God in a way that humans can understand. It is Jesus Christ, the Word of God, who is the source code of the Christian gospel. Therefore, "Thou shalt not restrict access to Jesus Christ, the Word of God."

What does this mean, practically? It means that Christians should avoid anything that hinders someone from being in relationship with Jesus Christ. This can be as simple as claiming that someone must hold a particular understanding of the life and ministry of Jesus Christ. It might also involve claiming that Jesus is only available to people of a particular race, gender, or sexual orientation. Or it might be as subtle and complex as equating Jesus with the dominant cultural understandings of what is good (that is, turning Jesus into an ancient proponent of modern free market capitalism).

However, it ultimately means that no one can claim to speak unequivocally for God or offer the last word on biblical interpretation. There are too many varied interpretations of the Bible, too many different religious traditions and theological expositions, and too many different communities of faith for any one person or group to be able to claim the one authoritative interpretation. If our relationship with the Word of God is dependent on one way of understanding the gospel, an understanding adopted at a particular time in a particular place by particular people, then it will be impossible to proclaim the incarnation of Christ to all times, all places, and all people. Yet, if we can recognize that there are many valid and valuable approaches to the freedom of Christ, we will find ourselves able to draw more fully on the gifts of God and be better prepared to offer freedom to others.

Criterion 3: Derived Works

The third criterion of the OSD guarantees the ability to create derived works. For a program to be considered open source, the developer must ensure that everyone is granted the right to modify the program for their own use and that they are granted the right to redistribute the modified work under the same terms as those by which they received it. The primary purpose of labeling software "open source" is to ensure that programs work for everyone. If my context requires that a program be able to perform a function not originally required by the author, then, according to the OSD, I am guaranteed the right to edit the software to add that function. Remember our story about Richard Stallman at MIT? If the printer software he was working with had been open source software, not only would there have been no need for him to request the source code from Xerox, but he also would have been free to edit that source code so that the printer program would have worked in his context.

Likewise, the gospel can and should be *contextualized* in order to be relevant to the time and place in which it is proclaimed. To ensure that the gospel's promise of freedom is heard, those proclaiming the gospel must be allowed to take advantage of and draw metaphors from the social context in which they find themselves. The way that I, as a pastor in Kansas City, proclaim the gospel is different from the ways in which my colleagues from other areas of the country proclaim the gospel, because here in the Midwest we have some particular ways of understanding how life works.

For example, have you ever listened to a person from Kansas talk about the Flint Hills? When most people think of Kansas, they think about I-70 and, as they pass through the glorious mountains of Colorado, they think about how long and boring that drive across Kansas was. In their very limited experience of our great state, they believe Kansas to be boring.

Yet the secret most Midwesterners know is that if you get off of I-70 about two hours west of Kansas City and then head south only twenty minutes, you will find yourself in some of the most luscious rolling hills you have ever seen. My wife likes to say that when you drive through the Flint Hills in the springtime, you would think that you had been transported to Ireland. This is a cheap example, to be sure, but preaching on the line from Psalm 23 about green pastures requires a lot less work when addressing central Kansas farmers than those in an urban setting who have never experienced acres and acres of lush green hills dotted with cattle.

A more substantive example of adhering to our third commandment, "Thou shalt celebrate the Incarnation by celebrating contextualization," would be to explore the ways different communities of faith gather and practice different disciplines of our faith. Again, a community of faith made up of primarily young adults who identify as artists and postmodern in their worldview will differ dramatically from that of our friends the central Kansas farmers. The "stuff of life" will be different for each of these communities. The questions these communities ask about the Christian faith will be different. The rhythms of life that each community practices will be different. For example, it makes sense for the farmers to hold Sunday worship midmorning, because early chores are done and lunch would not yet be ready. There is a natural lull in activity. But the young artists do not have that same rhythm to adhere to. While the farmers were up at 4:00 a.m., our artist friends might just be getting to bed. Many writings of the Bible will be easier for the farmers to hear and understand. Their industry and the industry of the Bible have much in common. Sabbath makes sense to a farmer when he reads of a people who were also agrarian, but how do we talk about Sabbath to a 24/7, wired-in generation? I don't know that answer, but it is going to be different for sure.

In addition, the ways in which I contextualize the gospel should not place restrictions on the ways in which another might contextualize the gospel. Neither our friends the farmers nor the urban artists have the right to say that their practice of Sabbath should be the norm for the other.

Celebrating contextualization means that we give thanks to God for the many ways in which the people of God live into freedom, and there will be as many ways as there are people of God.

Criterion 4: Integrity of the Author's Source Code

The first two criteria raise the questions, What is the purpose of being able to freely obtain a piece of software and have access to its source code? and Why give me the source code if I cannot put it to good use? The third criterion answers these questions and ensures that a user can in fact use the source code to modify a piece of software. Not only that, once the program has been modified, the "new" piece of software can also be freely redistributed in the same manner the original piece of software was.

One hesitation programmers had about distributing their software as open source was the fear that their work would be distributed with modifications that others might think was their original work. In some cases, the modification might reflect

poorly on the author, and this criterion was added to ensure that
modification could occur without the original author being held
responsible for derivations. To make clear the difference between
the original and the modified code, modified works must carry
a different name from the original.

If the church adequately meets the first three criteria of
this Christian reframing of the OSD, there will potentially be
countless contextualized understandings of who Jesus Christ is
and the purpose of his life and ministry. In fact, we can see that
there *already are* many understandings. An open source Christian
understanding will be comfortable with this, with one caveat:
No person or group should claim to possess the original, correct,
or sole understanding of the gospel.

It is not a big leap for a person to begin thinking that his
way of being a Christian is the best way. If he lives with this
belief for long enough, psychology suggests that his belief will
be reinforced to the point of believing that his understanding is the only legitimate one. This danger and temptation is
inherent in all lines of thought, including theological ones. An
open source Christian theology is no exception. Regardless of
our intent, because we are limited humans, we have shown
throughout history that we have a tendency to encourage our
own perspective and deny others'. As I will discuss in chapter
3, a lack of diversity is detrimental to the effective functioning
of a community, and one way to avoid that is to make sure our
various perspectives are honored.

When we obey the fourth commandment, "Thou shalt respect the integrity of the person and work of Jesus Christ," we
make clear to ourselves and others that we will never consider
ourselves to be in possession of the original, correct, or sole
understanding of Christ's person or work. This will encourage
us to seek out and celebrate other understandings of Christ's
person and work (the third criterion).

Criterion 5: No Discrimination against People or Groups

When considering who is to be included in the development process of a piece of open source software, the fifth criterion of the OSD is that there be no discrimination against people or groups. Once someone authors a piece of software and releases it (along with its accompanying source code) under an open source license, they give up their right to determine who can and cannot use, redistribute, or modify the software.

Let's say an author cannot stand left-handed people. If an author wants to restrict left-handed people from having access to their software and code, they are free to do so up until they release the program under an open source license. Once that is done, they have no right to restrict access to left-handers.

This criterion specifically addresses the software's license. When dealing with any piece of software, a *license* is the agreement between two parties, usually the author and those who would have access to the software for their (and others') use. The license sets out the parameters within which the program may be used.

Two convictions underlie this criterion. First, based on experience with the development process, those with an open source worldview operate out of the conviction that more people contributing to the process will translate into better software. Author and open source advocate Eric S. Raymond says it this way: "Given enough eyeballs, all bugs are shallow," meaning that the more people you have looking at a piece of software and its source code, the greater the chances are of someone finding an error and fixing it. These corrections can only happen this rapidly if the development process is dynamic and fluid and the source code is available to anyone at any time. By stating from the outset that all people and groups are free to be a part of the development process of a particular piece of software, open source authors are effectively saying that they believe all people have something to contribute to the process if they so choose.

The second conviction underlying this criterion is similar to the one that underlies the first criterion: developers of open source software should always bear in mind the long-term implications of their work. As Bruce Perens notes in the commentary to the OSD, "A license provided by the Regents of the University of California, Berkeley, prohibited an electronic design program from being used by the police of South Africa. While this was a laudable sentiment in the time of apartheid, it makes little sense today. Some people are still stuck with software that they acquired under that license, and their derived versions must carry the same restrictions. Open Source licenses may not contain such provisions, no matter how laudable their intent."[6]

In dictating that a certain group could not use a particular piece of software, the regents of the University of California, Berkeley, made a decision that affected multiple generations of South Africans. In this case, what appears to be a very good piece of software was forever hindered. It makes little difference that the "police of South Africa" are a radically different institution now from what they were during apartheid. The software license is clear: they are prohibited from using the software.

Applying this idea to the Christian faith means that no one can be excluded from receiving or proclaiming the fullness of the gospel. Even though a gospel whose goal is freedom would inherently require an openness to all people, the beauty of the gospel is most fully expressed when all people are able to bear witness to that freedom.

In mirroring the twofold conviction of the software criterion, an open source Christianity is also interested in having as many people as possible proclaiming the gospel in their particular contexts so that our understanding the gospel can be as full and faithful as possible. Open source Christianity is also interested in making sure that any expression of the faith is not limited by our current understanding but remains open to whatever it is God might reveal to us in the future.

Criterion 6: No Discrimination against Fields of Endeavor

The sixth criterion of the OSD is that there should be no discrimination against fields of endeavor. For software to be truly open source, it must be able to be used by anyone, anywhere, for anything. Just as some authors might not want certain people or groups using the software, other authors might not want their software being used for particular reasons. But this criterion prohibits software authors from discriminating against them.

For instance, an author may have a particular persuasion regarding abortion. They might develop a piece of software and decide that because they are pro-choice, they do not want their piece of software used by any person or group that would then use it to further pro-life purposes. Other people may want to restrict their software from being used to achieve particular economic goals. They may want to say their software can be used by nonprofit organizations but not by those seeking commercial gain. According to this criterion, you are free to use a piece of software for whatever purpose you wish.

In a similar way, an open source Christianity is committed to neither restricting nor inhibiting the actions of any person or group working to bring about freedom. Whether someone immediately resonates with the ministry or mission focus of a person or group, the intention of the gospel is to bring freedom in all its forms, and so all intentions that further freedom should be supported and celebrated.

I am personally opposed to several theological and ideological persuasions. However, since I have determined that the purpose of the gospel is freedom, if other Christians can demonstrate that the intention behind their ministry or mission is to bring about freedom for others, then as an open source Christian, I am obligated to honor their actions. I do not have to fully agree with them, but in accordance with the fourth criterion of the OSD, I cannot claim that my understanding of the gospel is a valid one while theirs is not. I should be humble enough to acknowledge that I might be wrong in my understanding.

It is perfectly acceptable, however (and a good exercise, at that), to engage others in conversation around the notion of *freedom*. Freedom should be the sole concern of an open source Christianity (since, again, it is the purpose of the gospel), and Christians should seek out, celebrate, and support any actions that further the freedoms of our fellow sisters and brothers. This is particularly important as we come into contact with stories of freedom that we find to be lacking. For instance, I often find myself troubled by stories that attribute the occurrence of a "turnaround" to a supernatural intervention. I can recall many stories of men who went to a revival meeting and stopped drinking the next day. I can recall many stories of people who claimed a "prayer of salvation" resulted in a complete change of behavior, so they were no longer the selfish person they once were. I know of many men who prayed fervently for the Lord to take away the feeling of lust in their hearts that had resulted in a pornography addiction and who afterwards were "free" from that habit. Yes, I find the "foxhole prayer," therapeutic-style theology that accompanies these kinds of stories deficient. I believe that a theology in which God is treated like a vending machine creates more problems than it seems to solve (Why did God choose to answer one prayer but not another?). But I have to ask myself whether a man free from alcohol, self-centeredness, and addiction is a good thing, and the answer is a resounding yes! And if these freedoms are found in the name of Jesus, I say, "Thanks be to God!"

Criterion 7: Distribution of License

The seventh criterion of the OSD addresses distribution of license. For software to be considered open source, the license accompanying a program must grant that the benefits of that license apply to all to whom the program is redistributed. There is no extra requirement (monetary or otherwise) that anyone must fulfill to be granted the right to use the software. As we have learned, a software's license is the agreement between (usually) two parties setting out the parameters by which the software can be used, and we have already established that the benefits of the license cannot be denied any person or group, nor can they be denied any person or group because of the intended use of the software. This criterion goes a step further to protect our free use of software.

Requiring upfront payment is not the only way that distributors make money from software. However, demanding upfront payment is a very direct method of closing off software. This criterion protects the user from being encumbered by additional requirements once the software is obtained, such as paying ongoing royalties or fulfilling certain behavioral agreements in order to be granted the benefits of the software. The annotated version of the OSD specifically forbids nondisclosure agreements. The author must release all of the code, not merely part, and that requirement must be met by any and all who use the software. (To be clear, software authors and distributors are more than welcome to establish nondisclosure agreements, but their works would not be considered open source.)

One exciting extrapolation of this criterion ensures that a person may receive benefits from the licensed software even if she consciously chooses to not use the software. Benefits are not behavior dependent.

I have a friend who is eighty-nine years old. Martha is one of the most well-read, well-educated people I have ever known. She is constantly reading and learning, seems to be up on the latest happenings of importance, and can always speak intelligently about them. However, she recently confessed to me that she has absolutely no desire to learn how to operate a computer, surf the Internet, or send and receive e-mail. "I'm an old woman," she says. "Even though my kids and grandkids want me to learn, I've lived most of my life without a computer, and I don't see why I need to begin now." I agreed with her and encouraged her to steadfastly refuse to use the computer if she didn't feel it would add much to her life. And yet, Martha benefits from the computer every day.

Every morning, for as long as she can remember, Martha exits her house, walks to the end of her sidewalk, and retrieves her newspaper. "That's all I need—that and the radio." I'm sure that Martha is cognizant of this, but *typesetting* and *laying out* the newspaper used to mean exactly that. It was someone's job to set the type into the printing press—arrange the blocks with each character on them. And someone physically, visually laid out the various elements of the newspaper, fitting them onto the page. Now, these tasks are all done on with a computer using programs designed specifically for those purposes. Whether Martha knows how to use these programs or even turn on the computers on which they run is irrelevant. She is benefiting from the software regardless.

In an open source understanding of Christianity, a software license is roughly equivalent to the covenant God has established with the people of God. When God first chose Israel, they were told, "I will be your God and you will be my people." Continuing on, the covenant that God has established through Jesus Christ adds understandings of the covenant unique to our religion. Jesus himself (quoting Isaiah) indicated that his disciples are to do what he did—proclaim in word and in deed the good news that all are free.

There is no work or action that one must perform in order to benefit from the freedom promised in Christ's gospel. Christ's gospel of freedom does not depend on someone regularly attending a worship service or educational offering or engaging in a missional experience. To be sure, those events will only help someone become more aware of their freedom, but they are not required as a prerequisite for experiencing freedom.

Criterion 8: License Must Not Be Specific to a Product

The eighth criterion of the OSD makes it plain that an open source software license cannot be specific to a particular product—a specific configuration of one or more pieces of software. This is intended to close off another potential avenue for limiting the freedom of the user.

Let's imagine you receive a product that is a suite of "office" software (OpenOffice, LibreOffice, Microsoft Office, iWork, for example). Within this bundle, you find three common programs—a word processing program, a spreadsheet program, and a presentation program. What this criterion ensures is that the three programs do not need to remain together for the open source license to apply. If, say, you find the presentation software woefully lacking in features and (rather than take advantage of the source code to modify it) you decide you would like to redistribute the word processing and spreadsheet program with a presentation program developed by another author, nothing could stop you from doing that. You do not need to keep the original configuration of the software bundle for the benefits of the license to apply.

In the same way, the freedom promised in Christ's gospel does not depend upon a particular understanding of that theology. Freedom is freedom, whether one has their theology "correct" or not. This is the place where I part ways, for instance, with sisters and brothers in Orthodox Christianity. I sometimes have heard that those of us who adhere to a form of the Christian faith other than Orthodoxy are somehow practicing a deficient form of faith. The claim is made (and I have no reason to doubt it) that the liturgy celebrated on a weekly basis has remained unchanged since the time of the early church. I find that fascinating and laudable, but I begin to be very disinterested (even frustrated and offended) when that same fact is used to claim that, for this reason, Orthodoxy is the "true faith"—the "right" way to practice Christianity.

I admit that this tendency is also found in the theologians of my own Reformed tradition. Reformed Christians are very logical people. Presbyterians in particular are known for their pride in doing all things "decently and in order." Naturally, we like our theology to be neat and tidy as well. We like mystery, but *messiness*? Not so much. As a result, Reformed theologians have produced some of the finest, tightest theological expression known to humanity. It is coherent, consistent, and cohesive. There is nothing that hasn't been accounted for. If you have ever had the fortune (or *mis*fortune, depending on your vantage point) of reading John Calvin's *Institutes*, Friedrich Schleiermacher's *Christian Faith*, Paul Tillich's *Systematic Theology*, or Karl Barth's *Church Dogmatics* (just to name a few classics), then you know well that Reformed theologians like to be exhaustive as well as precise. However, this produces not a small bit of arrogance on the part of theologians in my tradition. We are very proud of our work and seriously doubt that it can be done better. In my own church, the Presbyterian Church (USA), we even have a portion of our constitution that basically says, "We could be wrong about all of this, but don't count on it."

However, what is evidenced by both the Orthodox Church and the Reformed tradition is a sense that, unless you understand the work of God in Christ in a particular way, then you will not be privy to the benefit of freedom that the gospel promises. Nothing could be further from the truth, however. No theology, creed, confession, doctrine, or statement of faith can claim, or can be said to be vested with, a total embodiment of freedom. The totality of the gospel will never be found in a particular, contextualized expression of it. Acknowledging this is, in and of itself, a form of freedom.

Criterion 9: License Must Not Restrict Other Software

The ninth criterion of the OSD stipulates that the license must not restrict the functions of any other software. If a piece of software is going to claim to be licensed as open source, its license cannot stipulate terms or conditions regarding any other piece of software. To quote from the annotated OSD: "For example, the license must not insist that all other programs distributed on the same medium must be open source software."[7] In other words, the author of a word processing package cannot stipulate that it may only be used on computers on which all other programs are also open source.

While the desire to see wide adoption of open source software is a laudable, one goal this criterion makes clear is that the methods open source adherents use to achieve adoption must be consistent with our values. We cannot claim to promote openness and yet restrict the freedoms of others to achieve it. If freedom is the value that defines open source software, then that must mean we desire freedom for *all* software.

In a similar fashion, God's covenant with the body of Christ, while sufficient for an open source Christian, does not deny the truth and benefit found in other religious and wisdom traditions. We trust that the God who has given us freedom in Christ has acted to ensure the freedom of all creation. There is no need to say that our understanding of God's actions (revealed to us in the work and person of Jesus Christ) in any way limits or affects the truths of other religions.

An open source Christianity is not an exclusive one. Rather, it understands that the contextualized nature of God's work in the world extends farther than we may even be comfortable with. This is not to say Christians cannot bear witness to God in Christ to others, but it makes clear that our testimony is always tempered with humility. We can and should boldly proclaim a gospel of freedom as we have received it. (To not do so is to say that we do not think some person or group is worthy of freedom or in need of it.) And we should make clear in these discussions that freedom is our primary concern because we understand that freedom is the primary concern of God in Christ. However, our humility comes into play because we know that ours is not—cannot be—an authoritative representation of the gospel of Jesus Christ.

To proclaim Christ's freedom is to do so for all people—even if they actively deny that our gospel is effective and worthy of our proclamation. As I have said, one need not engage the covenant or license in order to receive its benefits. This understanding will aid us in our relationships with those in other religions and those of no religion. It will require us to be clear that our only desire is for their freedom and will allow us to continue in a relationship with them even if they reject the basis of our actions.

Criterion 10: License Must Be Technology Neutral

The tenth and final criterion of the OSD makes clear that open source software must be technology neutral, not limited to "any individual technology or style of interface."[8] The technology or style of interface that most people are familiar with are computers. Even if a program was originally created to run on computers using a version of the Linux operating system, when the software is modified to run on Windows and Apple systems, the same rights and benefits must still apply.

In an open source Christianity, we can understand "technology" (computers) as the rough equivalent of a church, a body of believers, because we understand the church to be a group of people called together by God to carry out God's purposes (as expressed in the source code, the Word of God, Jesus Christ). Even so, the establishment of God's covenant with the body of Christ is not determined by the existence or actions of a particular church or gathering of believers.

When I was younger, I was a member of a Southern Baptist congregation. I vividly remember a confrontation I had with a friend of mine one summer while living and working in Colorado. His family belonged to an *independent* Baptist congregation, and one day he began screaming at me (out of nowhere) that I might as well stop trying to live as a Christian because I was going to hell (!). "Even all these folks who don't go to church are better off than you!" I remember him yelling. His family had taught him that the church they attended and the form of faith they practiced was the only viable one. Salvation could not be found outside of that particular gathering of believers, and the fact that I was a member of a "rival" church made me worse off than unbelievers. Whereas they were ignorant of their situation before God, I was apparently actively working against a proper relationship with God. To him I was violating his understanding that one and only one "technology or style of interface" with the gospel of freedom was allowed.

Computer geeks argue all the time about which kinds of computers or operating systems are best. You are no doubt familiar with the Mac versus PC wars. However, for open source Christians, which is best is not even an issue. All gatherings of God's people have the potential to actualize the freedom promised. None are deficient.

An Open Source Church

In 1997 Eric S. Raymond presented a paper titled "The Cathedral and the Bazaar" at a conference for Linux developers. In this work Raymond presented the aphorism I quoted above: "With enough eyeballs, all bugs are shallow."

To demonstrate this thesis, he contrasted two different models of development, the cathedral and the bazaar:

> *The cathedral:* The source code may or may not be released with the final product, but during the development process, a select few people have access to the code.
>
> *The bazaar:* The source code is developed in full view of the entire world. Anyone who is interested can participate in the development process.

Raymond believes that the bazaar model is preferred to the cathedral model. Because a limited number of people have access to the code, those operating within the latter have to spend an inordinate amount of time searching for flaws and solutions. In almost all cases, the need to maintain a tight structure and exercise control results in a sacrifice of fluidity and flexibility. Raymond argues that this practice actually inhibits good development.

This book contrasts the cathedral and bazaar models as they apply to church. We all know what a "cathedral church" is, don't we? Even if our particular tradition doesn't have a structure called a *cathedral,* we have all had a church experience in which the "business of church" was controlled by just a few people. Any suggestion we might have made (if we even felt comfortable making one) was met with a less than enthusiastic response. The leaders of cathedral churches say "Trust us" a lot, don't they? You may or may not be told about the process of discernment those leaders went through to make decisions, but one thing is clear: when they say, "This is what we're doing," *that* is what you're doing.

But what does a "bazaar church" look like? What does it mean to say that the business of church should be opened up? What does open source church look like? I contend that we might gain helpful insight by taking a look at one of the most successful open source communities in existence: *Wikipedia.*

Chapter Two

Church as Wikipedia

At some level, the notion of a "Wikipedia church" makes a lot of sense—even if we have never thought of it before.

Wikipedia: The encyclopedia that anyone can edit
Wikicclesia: The church that anyone can edit

It kind of brings a smile to your face doesn't it? More important, it touches on a reality facing the church today: *Wikipedia* is a part of our everyday lives.

According to the Internet statistics aggregator Alexa Internet, every day 13 percent of the world's Internet users visit *Wikipedia* for some reason. At the time of this writing, *Wikipedia* was listed as the sixth most popular website in the United States and seventh worldwide. Thirteen million people worldwide are listed as registered users, and in the past thirty days, 135,000 of those users, on average, have edited an article on the site.

Wikipedia has become as synonymous with *encyclopedia* as Google has with *search*. The "wiki" phenomenon has caught fire, spawning many cousin sites, each dedicated to cataloging their own (often) niche corner of the world. (My personal favorite is Wookieepedia—the *Star Wars* Wiki).

Given this reality, how do we as the church expect to be the least bit appealing to people who increasingly go throughout their day knowing that they can "wiki it." Anyone anywhere can log on to the Internet and edit the world's largest encyclopedia. They can contribute to the "sum of all human knowledge," as *Wikipedia* describes it. They can offer their gifts of knowledge to the world and to generations to come. Yet we expect them to walk into our churches and simply take what's handed to them and do it the way we say they should? I don't think so.

Read a blog post, an article, or any number of books on emerging, emergent, or emergence Christianity, and you are likely to find some reference to Wikipedia in the text. It is increasingly becoming a popular metaphor for the way many would like to see the church structure itself and operate, but not a lot of time has been spent on the particulars of *Wikipedia* or why the project works as well as it does.

Let's Start Something for the Kids

Wikipedia didn't start out as the game-changer it now is. It started by playing second fiddle to another online encyclopedia, *Nupedia*.

According to the "History of Wikipedia" article on the *Wikipedia* site, *Nupedia* was viewed by its founders, Jimmy Wales and Larry Sanger, as a serious enterprise. This was to be a legitimate encyclopedia. Although it was to be a free online site, *Nupedia* was built on the idea of using contributors who were experts in their content area as well as the requirement that each article move through an extensive peer-review process. Wales and Sanger had a mailing list full of interested editors, with Sanger acting as editor in chief. They even had an intern. Yet the timeline for articles remained slow. In the first year, only twelve articles were produced. They needed a faster way to generate content.

Wikipedia began as a feeder for *Nupedia*. The intention was that articles would begin on *Wikipedia* and eventually be taken over by the *Nupedia* project to be cleaned up for inclusion in the "serious" online encyclopedia. To get the project up and moving, Sanger suggested the use of wiki (Hawaiian for "quick") software, which would allow collaboratively edited websites to be constructed. Sanger proposed the idea to the *Nupedia* mailing list:

> No, this is not an indecent proposal. It's an idea to add a little feature to Nupedia. Jimmy Wales thinks that many people might find the idea objectionable, but I think not. . . . As to Nupedia's use of a wiki, this is the *ultimate* "open" and simple format for developing content. We have occasionally bandied about ideas for simpler, more open projects to either replace or supplement Nupedia. It seems to me wikis can be implemented practically instantly, need very little maintenance, and in general are very low-risk. They're also a potentially great source for content. So there's little downside, as far as I can determine.[1]

Nupedia's editors were not excited about wikis being a part of their project, so *Wikipedia* was founded as a separate entity on January 15, 2001. By February 12, 2001, the project amassed one thousand articles; by September of that year, ten thousand articles; by its first birthday, twenty thousand; and by the next August, forty thousand.

Unfortunately, Wales and Sanger began to have severe disagreements about the management style of *Wikipedia*. Wales favored the open style that has come to define the project, while Sanger favored a more top-down approach (which eventually led him to leave the project and begin another online encyclopedia, *Citizendium*). This difference was seen by both men as intractable. Although ostensibly they shared the same goal (as *Wikipedia* would later say it: to ensure that every person on the planet has free access to "the sum of all human knowledge"), they had a sharp difference as to the best way to get there.

The *Nupedia* editors could not come to grips with the thought that a credible encyclopedia could be constructed in the wiki style. What they perceived as a rough-shod development process was an affront to the very thing they were trying to create—a resource that would make the best knowledge in the world available to everyone. How could that possibly be accomplished with *Wikipedia*?

Wikipedians, on the other hand, knew that "the sum of all human knowledge" had to come from somewhere and that as long as they could develop a system to harness it, they would be in good shape. By opening the doors for anyone to edit, they knew the combined knowledge of thousands—millions—of people would have powerful effect. Suffice it to say that what began as a project intended to benefit *Nupedia* quickly took on a life of its own and needed to break with its parent.

Even though there is not a firm one-to-one correlation between *Wikipedia* and an open source church, this brief history of *Wikipedia* provides us with our first point of comparison. If you are anything like me, you were part of a church experience during your youth that was fun and interesting, one where you thought you learned a lot and were valued for who you were. Your creativity was called upon, and you were encouraged to collaborate with others to a large degree. The thought seems to be that the church should do whatever it can to get kids interested in the faith, to make sure they understand that it is relevant to their life. In my denomination, the Presbyterian Church (USA), our national youth gathering is known to have some of the most creative, powerful worship that most staid Presbyterians have ever experienced. Yet there is a disconnect when our youth return to their congregations where little to no creativity is involved and efficiency is the order of the day. Our youth are discouraged from participating in worship because, in many cases, the service is simply a weekly puzzle. The pastor and musicians certainly put thought into the service elements, but the youth can't seem to get a good answer when they question why they can't sing a hymn in a different spot or why there can't be more, or fewer, hymns.

The message these youth receive is that when you become an *adult*, you begin to experience a very different form of church, one that is implicitly seen as more mature. "This is the way grownups do worship (or do missions, Christian education, and so on)." Given this sometimes jarring difference, are we honestly surprised that many youth leave the church and do not return?

In a similar vein, churches decide to start another worship service or what-have-you with the idea that this new program will serve as a feeder for the programming and structure they already have. There is an implicit understanding that this new thing is okay in order to get visitors hooked, but it will not be (cannot be?) the main thing. Church boards are okay with offering some new programs (or new spaces for programs) to attract young adults or young families, but I believe many of them harbor a strong hope that these new members will someday want to be a part of the church in the same way they have. They hope that these new people will want to continue developing and supporting the same organizational and programmatic structures that they have developed and supported over the years.

For some church boards the prevailing attitude is not hope but actually an arrogance that these young adults "will grow out of it." But most boards have a very real fear that they don't know what to do for young adults. So, they simply decide they are going to do what they have always done and do it well. The church they have known has served them well, so they will do all they can to preserve it and pass on what they understand as its strengths. They develop highly refined institutions and organizational habits. They are fine with this worship service where people wander around to prayer stations (but aren't prayers said together?) or the Bible study that meets in a bar (!), but at the end of the day "we all know the way church is done, really." In short—they act like ostriches (and Nupedia's editors) and stick their heads in the sand, hoping the desires of their young people will all just go away.

My point is not to harp on worship or Bible studies (or any one area of church life in particular) but to point out that what we have effectively been doing is trying to trick our youth and visitors into being a part of our congregational life by encouraging creativity and participation, only to then expect those same groups of people to "grow up" and begin supporting something that more resembles color-by-numbers and encourages us to sit back and be spoon-fed Jesus.

Wikipedia's origin story suggests to us what the church is in for (and has already experienced, in many cases) when it encounters an open source worldview. Established institutions are eager to do whatever they can to ensure their viability (*Nupedia's* development was slow, and *Wikipedia* would ensure that it got content up in a timely manner), but they rarely realize that the very thing they are counting on to save them will be the harbinger of their death. There might be a host of reasons for their demise, but the primary one has to do with structure. Institutions are generally aware that their current way of doing business is not tenable in the long run and are astute enough to know they must commit to some drastically different practices if they want to survive. But decades of habit are not easily changed.

At its most basic, the split between *Nupedia* and *Wikipedia* had to do with how and whether the site was curated. To put it another way: Who was in control? This will also be the issue that drives a wedge between established churches and their creative offspring. Those who resonate deeply with the established institutional form of Christianity will not really know what to do with more creative expressions. The very existence of alternative worship or educational experiences, in some cases, will be an affront to the very thing that established churches think they are about. Isn't the point of church to be a place where the Divine Truth is guarded and passed down from generation to generation? This cannot be accomplished by opening the doors and allowing anyone to contribute. Yes, we want contribution and participation, but there must be a measure of indoctrination first. You have to know how we do it before we will trust you to do it.

Yet, what if you come to the church with an open source view of the world? What if your entire life was one in which you experienced a collaboration of gifts, skills, and knowledge? What if, almost every day, you experienced the coming together of seemingly disparate voices and ideas that resulted in beautiful and tremendously effective and meaningful events and solutions? What if this was your world, and you then walked through the door of almost any church, where it quickly became apparent that your job was to sit down and shut up—that your job was to listen and be spoon-fed what you needed to think and believe? To ask the obvious question again: Why is it that I can edit the world's largest encyclopedia, but I can't edit church?

One cannot overestimate the role the wiki had on the trajectory of *Wikipedia*. The wiki allowed for real-time collaboration. Two minutes after an event happens, *Wikipedia* reflects it. There is no need to run something by a centralized authority figure. The infrastructure informs the ethos.

Likewise, one cannot overestimate the role an open, fluid, and dynamic church structure will have on the life of a congregation or regional body or national denomination. If we devise new forms of collaboration, it will necessarily lead to new understandings of community and ethics. As communication theorist Marshall McLuhan has famously said: The medium is the message. One can tell more about something based on the delivery vehicle than on what is actually delivered. If, week after week, I stand in my pulpit while wearing a clerical collar, large cross, stole, and a very impressive preaching robe, it doesn't matter that my message is, "You too can proclaim the word of the Lord." No one is going to believe me, because the medium of my particular presence there has told them the truth.

If we want to appeal to the "open source generation" (is there such a thing?), we can't be wedded to our current understanding of church structure. Our bureaucratic committee system will betray our true intentions, and that will repel those whom we hope to attract. I'm sorry, but it's true.

The Five Pillars

Probably the most common misconception about *Wikipedia* specifically, and open source in general, is that it promotes an "anything goes" mentality. As modern people, we have become so indoctrinated with either-or thinking that we assume the lack of a controlling bureaucracy is the only alternative. Nothing could be further from the truth. By definition, an organization without any organizing parameters is not an organization. Open source does not mean anarchy.

To be more accurate, open source means users can function with greater latitude. If you are used to an organization that has strict controls on this or that, you might, at first, be thrown by the freedom of an open source environment. But what you will quickly discover is that an open source organization still values some level of structure and clarity regarding purpose.

Wikipedia provides its users with parameters and purpose in the form of "The Five Pillars," which are the fundamental principles of the project.

WIKIPEDIA IS AN ENCYCLOPEDIA

The first of the Five Pillars makes clear why *Wikipedia* exists: "Wikipedia is an online encyclopedia and, as a means to that end, an online community of people interested in building a high-quality encyclopedia in a spirit of mutual respect."[2]

Of course, when anyone or any group defines what it is, implicit in that definition is what it *is not.* The *Wikipedia* community goes a step further to be very explicit in what it is not. An entire article has been written delineating (as exhaustively as possible, it seems) what the project is not,[3] but here is a summary from *Wikipedia's* main article on the Five Pillars: "Wikipedia is an encyclopedia. It incorporates elements of general and specialized encyclopedias, almanacs, and gazetteers. Wikipedia is not a soapbox, an advertising platform, a vanity press, an experiment in anarchy or democracy, an indiscriminate collection of information, or a web directory. It is not a dictionary, newspaper, or a collection of source documents; that kind of content should be contributed instead to the Wikimedia sister projects."[4]

It may surprise you to know that *Wikipedia's* goal is surprisingly narrow. Many good things need doing in the world, but those are not the concern of *Wikipedia.* If it does not have to do with ensuring that everyone has access to "the sum of all human knowledge," then *Wikipedia* (as an organization) is not going to bother spending energy on it.

To be sure, there are some things that *Wikipedia* must be concerned with, tangentially, in order to achieve their goal. In a speech to a TED conference,[5] Jimmy Wales noted that their goal means they must concern themselves with addressing the "digital divide," the very real, yet immaterial, chasm that prevents those in lower socioeconomic levels from having access to the Internet and most other technology. To *Wikipedia,* the "everyone" who needs to have access to "the sum of all human knowledge" is *everyone.* And so, even though working to develop digital access is not precisely developing an encyclopedia, the stated mission requires it.

That said, what does making clear "We are this and nothing more" do for *Wikipedia?* Simply, it guards against mission creep, that real situation many organizations find themselves in where they begin to pursue goals other than the ones originally stated. To be sure, something can be said for revising a mission, but use of the term *mission creep* implies that this expansion is not a good thing.

The best way to be successful is to maintain a single-minded focus on what is to be accomplished and to pursue that exclusively. Clarity is an organization's friend. If there is any confusion as to where energy or funds are to be directed, then the likelihood of an organization accomplishing *any* of its goals decreases dramatically.

Organizations should, first, be very clear about their mission and what they believe is required to ensure they accomplish that. Second, they must be vigilant against mission creep. Those responsible for fulfilling that mission need to constantly be asking, "Is this a part of our mission or not?" If there is even the slightest amount of rationalization that it is or should be, I suggest doing away with the idea.

So what is the purpose or mission of the church? If local congregations or regional associations or national denominations have any hope of being effective in the ministry God has given us, we must be clear regarding our purpose. I knew one pastor who used to regularly ask church committees some form of the questions, What do we have to offer that is uniquely the "church"? That is a great idea, but why should we be the ones doing that? What makes us different from the average social-service nonprofit?

The purpose of that line of questioning was to make sure congregational leaders were thinking about the unique gifts that we have to offer the world *as the church*. In my tradition, we look to what we call "The Great Ends of the Church," a list of six goals God has called the church into existence specifically to accomplish: "The great ends of the church are the proclamation of the gospel for the salvation of humankind; provide for the shelter, nurture and spiritual fellowship of the children of God; the maintenance of divine worship; the preservation of the truth; the promotion of social righteousness; and the exhibition of the Kingdom of Heaven to the world."[6]

To some, that list might look broad. To some, that list might look too narrow. But that is the list we Presbyterians go to when we are asked a questions like "What is the purpose of the church?" Of course, just like *Wikipedia*, tangential things have to be asked and attended to if the church is going to pursue those goals especially when we start to recognize that the church exists in many different contexts. What does promoting social righteousness look like for a national denomination? A regional association of churches? A local congregation? The answers to those three questions will most certainly look different, but the important thing is that they are answered.

My assumption is that all variations of the body of Christ called the church have some answer to the question, What is the purpose of the church? If not, then answering that question is the first step.

WIKIPEDIA HAS A NEUTRAL POINT OF VIEW

The second fundamental principle of *Wikipedia* establishes that the site advocates no singular point of view.

> Wikipedia has a neutral point of view. We strive for articles that advocate no single point of view. Sometimes this requires representing multiple points of view, presenting each point of view accurately and in context, and not presenting any point of view as 'the truth' or 'the best view.' All articles must strive for verifiable accuracy: unreferenced material may be removed, so please provide references. Editors' personal experiences, interpretations, or opinions do not belong here. That means citing verifiable, authoritative sources, especially on controversial topics and when the subject is a living person. When

conflict arises over neutrality, discuss details on the talk page, and follow dispute resolution.[7]

This pillar begins to suggest the reason many people disparage *Wikipedia*: the project is not concerned with getting to the truth.

When I speak about this book, I inevitably get asked a host of questions based on a person's perception that *Wikipedia* is (or can be or will be) full of false information: "What can you say about those times when *Wikipedia* is wrong? What good is an encyclopedia if we can't go there to find the truth about something?"

First, let's acknowledge the very real fear present in these questions: people want to know that the information they use in their day-to-day lives is reliable. We want to know that other people are not just making stuff up. Most of us are not comfortable in an anything goes environment. The reason, of course (at least, at some level), is that our lives depend on accurate information. An extreme example of this need would be the formulas used to calculate how gravity acts in our world and the propulsion needed for a plane to overcome its effects long enough for us to be carried through the air. No one wants to live in a world where someone can make up that kind of information up, do we? No, we want to live in a world where the science behind gravity is well established and consistently reconfirmed and verified.

But here's where the situation gets a little sticky: What if we're not talking about something so certain as gravity. What if we're talking about the city of Kiev in Ukraine? Were you aware of the dispute on *Wikipedia* about the spelling of that name? That, although the common English spelling is *Kiev*, in 1995 the Ukrainian government adopted *Kyiv* as the preferred spelling?

This may seem like a silly argument to you, but I can assure you that it is not to the Ukrainians. The "truth" of this matter is tied to national identity and ethnic history. How do you determine where the truth lies? I am certain that, as with most anything, one could find so-called experts and nonexperts alike who would testify to the validity of the argument they support. How do we decide? *Wikipedia* says we don't. Functioning as Wikipedians, we would do well to remember that it is not our job to make that decision, and here is where the second of the Five Pillars comes into play.

Wikipedia is not the vehicle through which to present cutting-edge research or wax on about your new theory on Ukrainian linguistics. *Wikipedia* is the place where all available information is brought to bear on the topic, and a group of people who care about it (presumably because of some connection to and knowledge of the subject) sift through it and make some sense out of it. Because some discrepancy in the information about the topic is likely, editors must cite *verifiable* sources for the edits they make. I may not like the edit you make, but if you can establish that there is at least a credible basis by which you made it, I cannot categorically revert the change. If I feel strongly enough about the change, I can begin a discussion on it in hopes of changing enough minds that I would be allowed to make the edit I want.

In the *Wikipedia* community, this approach is referred to as "verifiability, not truth." Remember, the stated goal of *Wikipedia* is to ensure access to "the *sum* of all human knowledge" (emphasis mine), not merely the pieces that a small group of people thinks are important. As long as I can validate that what I am contributing is established and credible, then I am free to contribute it.

This also means that seemingly competing pieces of information might appear side by side in *Wikipedia*. As we explored in chapter 1, the open source worldview that informs this kind of structure holds that we each inhabit different contextual realities. Your reality and mine will most certainly be different, but because we both have a valid basis on which to make our claims, we will need to learn to how to live with the tension. As of this writing, the English version of *Wikipedia* notes that the city in Ukraine is "Kiev or Kjiv." Both claims are present, because both can be verified.

To say that applying this line of thought to the church gives some people fits is an understatement. If you think that messing with someone's understanding of gravity or the spelling of Kiev/Kyiv makes them feel a little nervous and crazy, wait until you suggest that their theology might be treated in the same way.

Again, let's acknowledge the fear present in this thought: our faith is a very real thing that for many people is literally a matter of life and death. At some level, if our faith were not important, we would not waste our time on the question of truth. Just as with *Wikipedia*, we in the church aren't interested in an anything goes kind of environment. We want to know that the thing we are giving our life to is trustworthy and reliable. We want to know that when we come to know the truth that will set us free (John 8:32), we can count on that being the case. Nadia Bolz-Weber, Lutheran pastor and author of *Salvation on the Small Screen?*, likes to communicate that desire this way: we want to know that what we're involved in "is more than five minutes old."[8] Let's give ourselves some credit and say that, at our best, we are not arrogant people who think we can do this thing called the Christian life any old way we want. Especially for those of us in confessional forms of the faith, it would be the height of arrogance to assume we can say anything without being in conversation with what has come before us or is currently around us.

The problem we find ourselves in, however, is that there is much less agreement about certain aspects of our collective faith than there is about gravity. Besides the statement that "Jesus Christ is Lord," I am honestly not aware of a piece of Christian thought that doesn't more resemble the Kiev/Kjiv discussion.

An open source church asserts that there is not really a legitimate chance we are going to be able to truly know *the truth*, and we shouldn't try. Given the revealed nature of most versions of the Christian faith, I think we might feel comfortable enough to say that the truth has been revealed to us in Jesus Christ, but our previous discussion of context also makes plain to us that your experience (and subsequent explanation) of it might radically differ from mine.

So where does that leave us? What kind of church do we have at that point? If we view the church as similar to *Wikipedia*, what does it mean to assert that the church has a "neutral point of view"? I think it means two things:

First, when it comes to the church, what we're doing is passing on something equivalent to the verifiable information *Wikipedia* is interested in. The church is not a vehicle for experimentation when it comes to theology or practice. This suggestion might be off-putting to some, but this is not to say that other practices cannot be explored nor that theological exploration is not done.

An open source church will never say "We have the Truth," but it will say, "Here is what we have found to be reliable in many times and in many places." It's not "Believe this or you go to hell" but "If you want the abundant life, here's what we have found to be helpful."

Of course, the fun occurs when you and I begin discussing what exactly has been reliable over the ages. More often than not, we will find that we do not list the same things, which leads to the other point.

Second, an open source church will have space for different understandings to exist side by side. A classic example is the various understandings of atonement—of how and why Jesus's death and resurrection is the basis of our salvation. Some would say that God was paying the devil a ransom, while others would say that Jesus was taking the punishment that all of us should have had to endure for violating God's laws. Still others say that Jesus's death set us free from being bound to ourselves.

Which one is *the* truth? From an open source viewpoint, they all are, and they all will exist side by side in the church. We, of course, must demonstrate how these understandings and other practices are reliably conforming us to the image of Christ. However, once that bar is passed, it's just like *Wikipedia's* discussion about Kiev or Kjiv.

WIKIPEDIA IS FREE CONTENT

The third of the Five Pillars reminds us that *Wikipedia* is a project founded on and reflecting the open source worldview that I discussed in the first chapter. As such, it is established policy that anyone can use, edit, and distribute the content generated by *Wikipedia*. "Wikipedia is free content that anyone can edit and distribute. Respect copyright laws. Since all your contributions are freely licensed to the public, no editor owns any article; all of your contributions can and will be mercilessly edited and redistributed."[9]

Again, *Wikipedia* is not free for all or free rein in its organization. The process of building *Wikipedia* isn't anarchy but open source. If you quote a source (for verifiability purposes), you need to cite it. Open source does not mean that we ignore the models of organization that came before. It means that when we have the opportunity to create new models, we choose to make them more open. Plus, this pillar continues to remind contributors they are part of an encyclopedia project, not a project for cutting-edge research or opinion.

That said, users need to be aware that if they choose to contribute some content to an article, that content will likely be edited and changed. The work done by those who choose to edit articles is not for the benefit of any one person but for the "everyone" who needs access to "the sum of all human knowledge." Simply putting my heart and soul into an edit is not enough to warrant enshrining that work and freezing it for all eternity. If tomorrow something new is discovered on the subject, we should expect that the article will be changed again. Similarly, any contributor should expect that the work they do will be freely distributed. One should not contribute to *Wikipedia* expecting to be able to hold an article captive and limit access to it. Anyone across the globe can take advantage of the work anyone else does.

For the most part, no one has a problem with this pillar up to this point. They like the fact that they can edit an article because they, of course, know what they are talking about. They might have spent a good chunk of their life immersed in a given subject, and their contributions are going to be well founded and sensible.

The problem comes when someone makes an edit who is clearly not as knowledgeable on the subject as the first editor. Why should she get to make that edit? She doesn't know as much as I do, and she is being pretty presumptuous to think she does. What she needs to do is sit back and watch for a while to see how we do things, and *then* she can contribute!

I know this feeling of indignation intimately, even involving this piece of writing on open source (ironic, isn't it?). By the time this book is published, I will have spent almost four years of my life reading and thinking and constructing and synthesizing all sorts of information (ideas, stories, and more) on open source and Christianity. I will have put an incredible amount of time and effort into making sure that my thoughts are presented in a clear and consistent manner. If I do good enough work, someone might say that I could be considered an "expert" in the intersection of these two spheres. But does doing that work entitle me to claim that no one else can have a thought on open source and Christianity? Not at all.

The moment this book was published, it was out of date, and some new thought or idea was being generated that will eventually replace it. The moment I posted a draft of sample chapters to my blog, a strong possibility existed that some whippersnapper who has put maybe ten minutes of thought into the intersection of open source and Christianity might comment with the most cogent observation or idea that I—the "expert"—had missed entirely.

I tell you: That whippersnapper *did* show up (many of them!). I, personally, have already had to fight the feeling of protecting my baby, and this book is better for it.

Applying this pillar to the church highlights a tension that those who value a more open source church will have to address. The reality is that generations of history lie behind the conviction that the church should focus its efforts on preserving the institution, along with its accompanying traditions. An open source church will not share this conviction. Regardless of the benefits and effectiveness associated with the missions and ministries of one generation, an open source church will assume that each successive generation will add to and, in some cases, replace what came before them. They will take what they have inherited and use it toward new purposes. This will be as appealing to the established church as the use of a wiki was to *Nupedia's* editors.

We will find this tension to be especially pronounced in the mainline church. As author and pastor Jack Haberer points out in his book *Godviews,* unlike their evangelical counterparts, mainline churches are conservative not so much in their theology as they are in their structure. Whereas evangelical churches tend to emphasize the conservation of theological viewpoints but employ many structural models to communicate them, a mainline church will typically be much more comfortable with varying theologies yet resistant to various structures.[10]

One reason mainline churches feel hesitant toward the new is because of their tendency to record things. *Everything.* Those of us in mainline churches believe we have arrived at very good and workable solutions for many of the situations churches find themselves in, and we have written them down for future gen-

erations. This is a great impulse. For a while, I was the chair of
the committee who made sure that congregations in our region
kept their minutes appropriately, and I often told those in charge
(the clerks) that they were the foundation of the church. "If we
didn't have you," I would say, "we wouldn't know the giants
upon whose shoulders we stand."

But keeping such good records has a dark side, doesn't it?
Sometimes (often times?!) we end up resisting the movement
of the Holy Spirit, because, instead of intentionally considering
where God would have us go, we simply consult our past. "What
do the minutes say?" is a question I have heard often. Again, I
do not want to belittle the established institution but to locate
it in a particular time and place and remind us that we now live
(almost all of us) in a new time and place.

Think about *minutes* with me for a second. When you think
about a group recording its minutes, what do you think of physically? I bet all you good mainliners out there think of a beautiful
and meticulously kept book. Bound in leather with gold-em-
bossed lettering, the volume contains the record of the church's
history on thick archival paper. While the most recent entries
were generated with a laser printer, as you go back through the
decades you find typewritten pages before discovering page after
page of notes written in the most beautiful penmanship you
have ever seen. When you look at those earlier pages, you are
struck not only by their content but also by the fact that some
faithful soul sat down month after month and wrote them out
by hand. If you're the sentimental type, you might even shed a
small tear and thank God for her, commenting how you could
never handwrite minutes for long before your fingers started
to cramp.

In the era of handwritten minutes, a lot of value was placed
on those pages—their accuracy and the truths they contained.
The minutes were almost scriptural in their status, because they
represented (for all intents and purposes to a local congregation)

the authoritative word about what a church felt its call from God was. If those clerks or secretaries were worth their salt, just as much effort was given to the beauty of the page as to their content. Having to cross out a line, I am sure, would have been insulting. Nearly all of these understandings carried over into the typewritten era, which merely added the idea that we can be efficient in discerning and recording the truth.

But now think about the age of *Wikipedia* and digital recordkeeping. True, wiki programs have a feature that will show someone a previous draft of the document, but (for the most part) when a line is corrected in a digital format, the new replaces the old, and the old is no more. If I were to delete and replace this sentence as I type it into my laptop, it ceases to exist for anyone but me. Only I know what that sentence said.

I am not trying to advocate one method of recordkeeping over another. Rather, my intent is for us to recognize that the *technology* we use to live our daily lives influences how we see the world and the way it operates. It is also important to recognize that this is not limited to our individual lives but applies to our collective lives as well. To say that the church must learn from *Wikipedia* is actually not just a fun mental experiment. Rather, it is to say that *Wikipedia* serves as an example of the technology that has informed the lives of an entire generation and should, therefore, inform the way in which the church interacts with this generation.

To an "open source Christian," to be a part of a community in which nothing can be changed is uninteresting at the very least and offensive at worst. This fact may not bother you. Your first reaction might be one of sarcastic pity—"Oh, those *poor little babies* who don't get to do whatever they want. How sad for them." But I would encourage you to rethink that reaction. Those who view the world through an open source lens are often those under thirty-five years old, and this is a group of people who are increasingly leaving our congregations, never to return.

They have no interest in being a part of a community that does not value their contributions. Actions that you consider to be a way of passing on a legacy they consider to be methods of top-down command and control.

An open source church will embrace the belief that God has gifted all people and will structure itself so that they can participate in the same way *Wikipedia* encourages anyone to edit. An open source church will live out this belief in celebration, knowing that, just as with past generations, God will be able to use the understandings of each subsequent generation to accomplish peace, justice, and wholeness.

WIKIPEDIANS SHOULD BEHAVE IN A RESPECTFUL AND CIVIL MANNER

As I have stated repeatedly, many people believe that *Wikipedia* is simply an experiment in anarchy. In fact, the fourth of the Five Pillars places an expectation on Wikipedians that they will act appropriately in times of disagreement and conflict: "Wikipedians should behave in a respectful and civil manner. Respect and be polite to your fellow Wikipedians, even when you disagree. Apply Wikipedia etiquette, and avoid personal attacks. Find consensus, avoid edit wars, and remember that there are 3,393,351 [at the time of this writing] articles on the English Wikipedia to work on and discuss. Act in good faith, never disrupt Wikipedia to illustrate a point, and assume good faith on the part of others. Be open and welcoming."[11]

It makes sense that if an organization has a policy to open up its workings to most anyone, then *anyone* is exactly who will come and participate. With this kind of policy, an organization has effectively forfeited the right to determine who can and cannot participate in a project based on any kind demographic criteria (or what my mentor used to call *accidental characteristics*). When a diverse group of people gathers to work on a project, they are going to have varying ideas not only about what the project can or should be but also about how to accomplish their goal. No one is going to agree 100 percent of the time with everyone else, and conflicts will naturally arise. Some will be taken care of very easily (they might be the result of a very minor misunderstanding), but some will not. The Fourth Pillar offers guidance to the community for these "some will not" situations.

I like to state the basics of *Wikipedia's* conflict management advice this way: *Act on the trust that everyone wants the best for the project, and they will do the same for you.* True, at times people will act selfishly, and, true, at times the whole idea of an open source project on the scale of *Wikipedia* will look foolish. This is unavoidable, because there will always be people who will take advantage of another's trust. But the conviction of *Wikipedia* is that the benefits of trusting your fellow editors far outweigh the benefits of spending copious amounts of time and energy ensuring that no one can deceive you. Wikipedians would rather spend their time reminding one another of the good that comes from a system of trust than enforcing rules that would denote a system of fear and litigation.

Because an open source church commits itself to being as open as possible, it also commits itself to cultivating and maintaining a high level of trust. An open source church understands that the more open an organization is, the more it must practice trust. These practices might look different from congregation to congregation, but they are all based on the belief that, even though people of goodwill will disagree, assuming that the other person is acting in the best interest of the group will go a long way to solving problems. To assume that the other person is always trying to deceive us will only result in an impasse.

Once, someone asked Jesus how many times he had to forgive his brother. Jesus responded, "Seventy times seven" (Matt. 18:22). All the nuanced interpretations aside, the point Jesus was making was, "You can't forgive someone too much." In his second letter to the Corinthians, Paul made the case that God in Christ has given us "the ministry of reconciliation" (5:18). He said that, in God's own actions through Christ, creation was reconciled to God, and our mission was to carry on that work. In both instances, trust is paramount.

Both cases deal with some form of estrangement—situations in which two people have been separated or drifted apart. The way forgiveness is made real by one brother to another is for the one who was wronged to communicate that he trusts his brother will not wrong him again, setting up an expectation for the way they will relate to one another going forward. The way reconciliation is achieved is for two sisters to trust that whatever has driven them apart does not have to define their relationship forever. This will require telling and listening for the truth on both of their parts, and perhaps some forgiveness. But, ultimately, trust is what allows them to come together.

The Fourth Pillar of *Wikipedia* reminds users that they have millions of other things to focus on (namely articles needing attending to!), so the community does not have time to waste on fighting. The same goes for the church. Millions of people and situations need freedom brought to them. We do not have time to fight among ourselves when God has called us to such an important task.

WIKIPEDIA DOES NOT HAVE FIRM RULES

The fifth of the Five Pillars codifies the understanding that *Wikipedia* is still, at its heart, an open organization, subject to change: "Wikipedia does not have firm rules besides the five general principles presented here. Be bold in updating articles and do not worry about making mistakes. Your efforts do not need to be perfect; prior versions are saved, so no damage is irreparable. However, don't vandalize Wikipedia."[12]

Ultimately, *Wikipedia* makes the trust encouraged in the Fourth Pillar an official policy. Trust is not simply a good idea for the Editors to remember as they interact with one another, but it is such a good idea that the organization itself has built into its DNA the belief that sometimes good policies, procedures, and schedules need to be thrown out to make things better. If Editors did not trust one another, there would be countless detailed prohibitions that everyone would have to abide by.

Many organizations have an extremely detailed manual of operations that instructs them on what to do in almost any eventuality. If a situation arises, a process to address it is in the book! This level of detail does not happen overnight, but over time. Someone suggests a *best practice* and, because it seemed to work this time, they conclude it must be a good idea for all time. It is written down and voted on; it is made an official part of the way the organization does business. Initially, having this best practice as a part of the official operating procedure may not be a problem, for this practice very well could be a fantastic way of tackling a given problem. However, issues arise for organizations when they are wedded to the successful way things have been done in the past and not open to discovering creative and intentional solutions for today (which might very well resemble past ones).

When organizations are wedded to the past, they typically try to solve whatever problems come up by shoehorning them into existing solutions. They may have a high tolerance for this kind of activity because these moments are probably few and far between. Yet there are a couple of ways in which confidence in "business as usual" can begin to erode.

One is that problems start coming faster and faster, and it becomes clear that operational procedures need to be changed to accommodate them. For the organization's sake, it is best if these problems come so fast and are so varied that all faith in the old strategies is abandoned and replaced by an approach that addresses each problem in turn, drawing upon the present strengths of those in the community to come up with creative solutions.

The second way in which confidence in business as usual begins to erode is when those in charge simply find people to carry out preassigned duties. We live in what emergent author and pastor Doug Pagitt calls an "inventive age." People do not want to be recruited to produce widgets. The era of recruiting people to fill slots is over. People want to contribute through their own creativity, and so, when they are contacted yet again to be a cog in someone else's machine, they refuse. When enough people refuse, those in charge begin to see that their procedures must change.

If an open source organization understands anything, it understands that the more you dictate process, the more you strangle creativity and innovation. In *Wikipedia's* case, those who choose to edit an article are encouraged to be bold in their actions. Be bold, or be quiet! Go big, or go home! Be attentive to the way things are normally done, but if you think that something you can do will better ensure that everyone has access to "the sum of all human knowledge," do it. Take risks, knowing that you will most likely fail often. The reason *Wikipedia* can operate like this is that, if something doesn't work, things can always be put back the way they were. Everything is saved; nothing is lost.

Can we be honest that this approach scares the crud out of most people in churches? For some reason we are risk averse in the church, and we like it that way. I think some of our aversion to risk comes from a lack of understanding about the church's purpose. As I said earlier, there are many ways to answer the question, What is the purpose of the church? but if the church at all levels is faithful, all the answers will involve creatively working for the peace, justice, and wholeness of God's creation. Another reason for the risk aversion is that many of us just don't want to spend a lot of time on "church things." It is seemingly easier to maintain what we've got going on than to put time and energy into revising. Still another reason might be that changing things is a tacit admission that we don't know what we're doing. If we stay the course, we tell ourselves, we might at least appear to be competent.

I believe one of the most significant reasons for our aversion to risk comes from our understanding that we are a law-abiding people. To a large degree, we see risk as actions that go against the ways we have agreed we will all behave. Whether in religious or civil situations, we believe ourselves to be people who are guided by the idea that certain things are fixed—there is a right and there is a wrong. All we have to do is figure out the proper way to embrace one and avoid the other. To that end, our sets of rules and guidelines, our minutes and manuals of operation, serve as a way for us to keep from straying off the right path. We trust that those who have trod this path before us have been faithful and that the procedures and parameters left to us are commensurate with what God expects of us. However, this line of thought mirrors the one that the Second Pillar tries to address: the reality of various points of view. Just as the Second Pillar reminds us, regarding *content*, that we must be attentive to the varieties of truth present in the world, the Fifth Pillar wants us to expand that attentiveness to include our *processes*.

As our survey of an open source worldview reminds us, varying times and places require varying ways of doing God's work. The church must be willing to be contextual and translate the word of God for the places in which we find ourselves. We won't get it right the first time, but we shouldn't worry: we always have time to improve our work, and we can go back to our old methods if we need to.

Who's Who?

Speaking about foundational principles and guiding ideologies is easy, but they are functionally irrelevant unless actual people live by them. An organization is defined not by principles, policies, and procedures but by people coming together to accomplish a particular goal. A structure is useless unless it is populated by people who can take advantage of the structure and put it to use.

The success of any organization is defined (in part) by clarity about who plays what role. In a traditional hierarchical organization, organizational roles are usually arranged like a pyramid, with *the most important person*—the "boss"—at the top. Everyone else in the organization functions, to some extent, to support the vision of the boss. The boss may have inherited a set of goals from a previous boss or from a board, but the vision of the way forward ultimately depends on this one person. Everyone else is "support staff."

As an open source organization with the Five Pillars as its guiding philosophy, *Wikipedia* does not place one person at "the top," making them solely responsible for accomplishing the goal. *Wikipedia's* model is to flip the pyramid, giving *the most important position* to its users. Rather than the majority of the people in the organization supporting the vision of one person, *Wikipedia* asks a smaller group of people to perform certain functions for the good of the majority of people involved in the project.

For the purposes of our thought experiment, four basic roles in the *Wikipedia* community are applicable to the life and ministry of an open source church. The first two shed light on the most basic category of involvement in any organization: *membership*.

One role is as *Wikipedians*. This group encompasses the users referred to previously. More formally called Editors, those who contribute in any way to *Wikipedia's* stated goal of ensuring that everyone has access to "the sum of all human knowledge" are considered members of the *Wikipedia* community. *Anyone.* You are a member of the community by virtue of your participation in the community. There are no hoops for you to jump through. If needed, you are educated about the Five Pillars, but—mostly—you're left to take advantage of the structure of *Wikipedia* and to offer the wealth of specialized creativity that you possess.

A second role is *Registered Wikipedians.* Wikipedians in this group have taken the step to set up an account on *Wikipedia.* The difference between an Editor and a Registered Editor is minimal, even though it is significant. Whereas an Editor can only edit the content of an article, a Registered Editor can start an article, upload images, rename articles, and take advantage of advanced editing tools. Although not everyone chooses to do so (I have not), being a Registered Editor of *Wikipedia* affords someone a more full experience of contributing to the project's goal.

When they were conceived, most current official categories of church membership were intended to serve administrative and financial functions. In the Presbyterian Church (USA), the 1806 General Assembly adopted a policy that the lower levels of the denomination would pay for the expenses of its assembly commissioners through an annual per capita (meaning "by head" or "by person") financial apportionment. This action mirrored earlier actions by regional groups of churches (1734) requiring them to accurately determine the number of heads in its member churches, and the idea of official membership was born. Even though churches have learned to reflect on membership theologically, the idea is still rooted in an organization's need to support and perpetuate itself. If the church were to use the two roles provided by *Wikipedia* as the basis for our understanding of membership, I believe the functioning of our congregations and denominations would look radically different.

Whether or not we are aware of it (let alone admit it), the main reason most congregations strive to attain new members is to bolster the bottom line. Individuals and families are often referred to as *giving units*, and even though those in charge of fund-raising tell us that the construction makes it easier to assess the budget a board can put together, it ultimately affects the way in which we view those in our pews: they are there to provide capital for our programs. This ultimately affects the ways in which we promote ourselves to the community, up to and including where we send advertising materials. When a congregation has limited amounts of money to spend on mailers, they find that they want to *maximize the return* on that investment, so they target "growing" areas or areas with a lot of young families. I have never encountered a congregation that has sent mailers to the poorer sections of their town, and if there is one, I suspect that it is a rarity. I point this out not to make us feel guilty but to make clear that our underlying understanding of membership affects many decisions we make in our congregations.

Although I have heard stories, every church I know of welcomes most everyone who walks through its doors, even if they haven't sought them out. They greet them and invite them to be a part of the life of the community (whatever that might be) with the hope that these visitors will eventually want to become *members*. If they do choose to join, we lead them through some sort of initiation process, and they are received into the membership of the church. And then what do we do with them? We *wait* for them to get involved. Why do we do this? Usually it's because we want to make sure we do not burn them out, because if we do, they will leave, and if they leave they won't tithe, and then how will we pay for our building and programs? This is exactly the kind of thinking born of an understanding of *members* as those who provide resources. This kind of thinking leads us to assume our pastors or church boards are the people "at the top" whose vision the membership is supporting.

In truth, those who come to our churches are doing so because they want to be a part of an organization that will enable them to serve something beyond themselves. They want to be more than giving units.

Recently I contacted a new couple in our church to ask if they would mind leading the youth group. They had been worshiping with us for about nine months and had formally joined the church two months before I extended my invitation. I wrote them and explained that some shifts in my job responsibilities were going to make it difficult for me to continue being the lead youth person, that I normally hated to ask new folks to take on significant responsibility, but would they mind? The next day I got an e-mail from them saying, "Yes. We actually wanted to volunteer, but weren't sure if that was okay or needed." I was simultaneously thrilled and embarrassed. I, too, had succumbed to the idea that members were content to provide resources and back up someone else's vision.

Yet, what this little episode taught me was that, although this couple had spent seven months contributing to the life of our community in whatever way they were comfortable, when they decided to formally align themselves with our congregation, they expected to be involved and contribute the gifts and skills that they had. In them can be seen the functions of *Wikipedia's* Editors and Registered Editors. For seven months, they were fine to participate in this church clean-up day or that caroling to the shut-ins; and when they formally joined as members, they did so wanting to play a larger role in the congregation. The tragedy is that if we had not had an immediate need, our understanding of membership might have shut them out.

The third and fourth roles of the *Wikipedia* community, Administrator and Benevolent Dictator, help us reassess our understanding of leadership roles in the life of our churches. Once a Wikipedian has been a Registered Editor for a period of time, they can be chosen by the community to function as one of a variety of *Administrators*. These people can delete articles when called for, roll back articles to previous versions, block users, and so forth.

In short, these are individuals trusted by the community to use certain tools to keep the community and its work running smoothly. They might still contribute to *Wikipedia* as a Registered Editor, but in their role as Administrator, they agree to perform certain watchdog functions for the sake of the group. In the understanding of *Wikipedia*, the privilege of being able to use these tools does not make an Administrator better or more important than anyone else. It simply recognizes that they are trustworthy enough to serve the community as a whole. If an Administrator weighs in on an issue, their status as Administrator should carry no weight, and they should never insist that it does. In fact, the symbol for *Wikipedia's* Administrators is a mop, and they are often referred to as the "janitors" of the community. They clean things up and make sure the project functions smoothly for everyone.

This understanding of leadership is actually quite commensurate with many Christian traditions. In my own, when we ordain and install elders, deacons, and ministers, we say that God has called them and "set them apart, not above" for service to the church. Do our churches' leaders think of themselves as janitors or executive vice presidents? Do they understand their job to be that of housekeeping or running the show? This simple distinction is really the impetus for this book. Even though our theology of leadership is sound, we often act in ways quite contrary to it. While we say that we believe God has called each person to mission and ministry, the organizational structures we have created actually discourage people from pursuing their call in favor of the institution's goals. I do not want to suggest that everyone is a natural born leader, but I am suggesting that our organizational structures dramatically underestimate the number of natural leaders sitting in our pews. If we believe that God has called and gifted individual members to engage in certain ministries, what is the most effective way to support the ministry of these individuals in our communities?

I will return to this subject in the next chapter, but I want to submit now that unleashing the creative force that is the congregation will require two things: first, a change of heart and a different understanding on the part of church leadership, from being in charge to housekeeping; second, a change in organizational structure that encourages and rewards members' creativity and innovation while discouraging and punishing leaders who use their positions to unduly influence the process of ministry. While we hope and pray that leaders will always use their tools and privileges for the community's well-being, we cannot solely depend upon them to behave perfectly in every situation. These two changes will communicate to other members how leaders are to function, and they will serve as a safeguard that prevents leaders from abusing their positions. Even people of good intent sometimes make horrible mistakes, and an official and regularly communicated understanding of who plays what role will deter most transgressions.

In open source communities, someone almost always fulfills the fourth role, *Benevolent Dictator* (BD). At first glance, the term seems to combine two mutually exclusive ideas, and those in the open source world use it with a large measure of irony. Although the BD is a person with almost unlimited power to take unilateral action (a dictator), it is commonly understood that this person can never exercise that power for his or her own self-interest or benefit, or for the interest and benefit of a small group of people. BDs should always exercise their power in a way that benefits the entire community (should be benevolent). The BD functions as the chief protector of the community, sometimes even protecting it from itself. Because of the openness of open source communities, it is understood that the BD's power is given at the consent of those being "governed" and can just as easily be taken away.

In the *Wikipedia* community, founder Jimmy Wales serves as BD. He is listened to in ways that others are not and expected to continually make sure the community is aware of its vision and goals. At times Jimmy has used his power to protect the community. When a rash of vandalism by neo-Nazis once occurred, the community was worried that their open process would be sabotaged precisely because of its openness. However, because no one was in charge, no one had the authority to do anything about it. Except Jimmy.

In relating this story to a TED conference,[13] Jimmy told of how he understood his role—as the one person who can protect the community's openness. In dealing with the neo-Nazis, he blocked several users and locked down several articles until the issue abated. Jimmy used his extraordinary power to protect the project from being derailed. But he usually operates in the same ways that any normal Registered Editor would. He does this because the organizational structure of *Wikipedia* (which includes its open source license) all but requires him to. If he did not use his extraordinary power benevolently (and then only sparingly), nothing would stop the user base from taking the content of the site to start a separate project *without Jimmy*.

Leaders of this stature, by virtue of either their longevity and dedication or their role in the community, are present in our congregations. Occasionally, the BD of a congregation is a longtime member who has served the church selflessly and well, but the person who typically fills the role for a congregation is its pastor. Just like Jimmy Wales, pastors are no more special than any other member, but by virtue of their role in the congregation, they are afforded a massive amount of power. Also, just as with Jimmy, nothing prevents members from leaving a congregation if a pastor abuses the authority given to him or her.

I submit that pastors (and certain other leaders in the church—other staff, clerks, secretaries, and treasurers come to mind) must learn to see themselves as Benevolent Dictators, subject to the consent of the "governed." Their role is to provide the community in which they serve a constant and consistent view of the vision and goals of that congregation and to use their authority to protect the flock as a shepherd would when people or events threaten to jeopardize mission and ministry. As Jesus himself reminded the disciples, it is those who do not know God who have leaders who flex their authority. "But it is not so among you," he said, "but whoever wishes to become great among you must be your servant" (Mark 10:43).

The Proof of the Pudding

As I stated at the beginning of this chapter, even though the idea of a Wikipedia church—a church anyone can edit—might bring a smile to our faces, there will still be those of us who feel hesitant to invest in it. No one is going to blame you for that feeling. Ultimately, we have been gathered together as God's people to participate in the mission and ministry God has set out for us. As I have already suggested, as Christians none of us shows up week after week simply to play church. We truly believe that God has called and gifted us, and we want to be as faithful as we can be.

And so we are not going to simply abandon the church organizational structures that have served us well for decades and that saw Christianity reach levels of influence previously unknown. A mere generation ago, a staggering percentage of the population in the United States not only identified as Christian but also attended some sort of worship service on a weekly basis. It was these organizational structures that led to what has affectionately became known as "The Christian Century." To propose the open source church is not to say that the traditional, hierarchical church is bad or ineffective. It is to say that worldviews change and so structures must do the same. As much as a Wikipedia church is about a way of understanding, in the end it is even more about a change in structure.

All the same, if something works, then it works, and so we must now turn our attention to whether or not this open organizational structure can, in fact, work. As the old saying goes, the proof of the pudding is in the eating. How does the open source pudding taste? Can we employ the insights and ideas of the Open Source Definition and *Wikipedia* and still accomplish the work God has called us to? I believe that we not only can but that, if we draw upon the wisdom inherent in crowds, we will also find that our ministries will more effective.

The Wisdom of Crowds

In his book *The Wisdom of Crowds*, author and *New Yorker* magazine columnist James Surowiecki reminds us of the phenomenon that was *Who Wants to Be a Millionaire?* According to Surowiecki, several times a week the popular game show presented us with an opportunity to watch individual intelligence compete against group intelligence. And, as he notes, "every week, group intelligence won."[14] One of the key aspects of the game was that contestants were given several "life lines" designed to help them answer a particular question and move to the next level of play. Two of these life lines allowed them to either phone a friend or ask the audience.

Everyone who watched the show had their list of who they would call if they became a contestant: Aunt Sally for anything having to do with the arts; your best friend Dominic would be the obvious choice when it came to pop culture; your dad for current events; and your brother for sports-related questions. These were the people you knew who were experts in these areas. You were confident that you could call them with just about any question, and they would be able to answer it. They were able to do so in normal, everyday life, so why not on a show?

Over the course of the show's run, these "experts" did, in fact, do okay, offering the right answer—under pressure—almost 65 percent of the time. But they paled in comparison to the audiences. Those random crowds of people with nothing better to do on a weekday afternoon than sit in a TV studio picked the right answer 91 percent of the time.[15] To be sure, the results from *Who Wants to Be a Millionaire?* wouldn't be admissible in court, but what Surowiecki demonstrates with this example is a well-documented phenomenon at the heart of his book: *groups of normal people can consistently discern better solutions than an expert.*

Millionaire audiences were unlikely to get tripped up, because the audience members' wide range of knowledge meant that they were able to approach problems from several different vantage points and employ information from several different areas. And, while we think that it is impressive when people are answering a simple question on a game show, we will soon see that the wisdom of crowds is even more pronounced when a group of people tackles a complex issue requiring a multistep solution— something church boards are called upon to do regularly.

Surowiecki claims that a group of normal people can outperform an expert almost every time if the following four conditions are met: diversity, independence of thought, decentralization, and aggregation of collective wisdom.

DIVERSITY

As we will see, the more similar a group is, the greater their chances are of attaining a high level of cohesiveness. However, cohesiveness lulls a group into insular thinking and shields it from outside, alternate thinking. The result is groupthink. If a group is to be wise rather than merely cohesive, members will be diverse in their opinions, beliefs, life experiences, race, class, gender, and education level. Even one divergent opinion or one person asking simple, probing questions will make a group smarter.

The *Millionaire* crowds were made up of random groups of people who all happened to be in the same place on the same day. They represented a fairly varied cross-section of people with different life experiences, opinions, and education levels. Because they each lived different lives, they each had different gifts and skills. Likewise, by allowing anyone to edit, *Wikipedia* is codifying a method for ensuring as much diversity as possible.

INDEPENDENCE OF THOUGHT

Almost every group has a member or two who tends to dominate conversations. Because these individuals are so persistent in their opinions, other group members gradually begin to subordinate their ideas and opinions. This sets up a dynamic in which an "expert" is again established, nullifying whatever diversity has been achieved.

The *Millionaire* crowds don't get to talk to one another. The only thing they can do is press their keypad. There is no chance for them to be influenced by the woman on the other side of the room who is certain that she knows the right answer.

Wikipedia's commitment to maintaining itself as an ency-clopedia and its insistence on a "neutral point of view" and verifiable information help to ensure that individuals who have access to relevant information are able to contribute it without being forced to conform to an ideology.

DECENTRALIZATION

Many organizations make the mistake of insisting that all deci-sions either be approved by or—worse yet—originate with one person or group. The thinking goes that if one person or group serves as the clearinghouse, then it will be less likely that something *irregular* happens. Yet this person or group rarely has the knowledge of the situation that someone closer to the ground would have. Two things result: workflows become bottlenecked and the organization begins to become passive, deferring instead to its recognized experts. The reality is that allowing specific individuals to apply their knowledge to the areas they know best is the most effective way to accomplish any goal. To create a culture of decentralized action that is at the same time consistent with the larger vision, a basic set of norms and expectations must be set up and promoted.

For the *Millionaire* crowds, the process for giving answers was tailored so that each audience member could offer their information simply and directly. They didn't have anyone checking their work. They didn't have to run it by anyone. They just voted.

Wikipedia establishing its Five Pillars and encouraging its Editors to be bold with editing helps to meet this condition. By setting out clear expectations and expecting users to be highly independent, decentralization becomes a reality.

AGGREGATION OF COLLECTIVE WISDOM

Paradoxically, what is required to ensure that a diverse, independent, decentralized organization can complete its work is a small amount of centralization in the form of *aggregation*. Even though an open organization wants to maintain decentralized action, it also wants to be able to maximize the efforts of everyone involved. This is accomplished by making sure that the work of various parts of the decentralized system is available to the other parts.

The independent, decentralized information offered by diverse *Millionaire* crowds was aggregated by the computer system that received their votes. This aggregation was then projected on a screen for the contestant to see and use as he or she saw fit.

Wikipedia's system of aggregation is in the form of the software itself—the wiki—as well as those tasked with maintaining the usability of the wiki, the Administrators. As an Editor goes about her work, she uses the format of the wiki to add to the collective wisdom of the project. The Administrators of the community use the tools at their disposal to make sure that the work of the Editors can be as smooth as possible. Those given the responsibility to do so guard the process, and in the rare case when something happens that is outside the scope of an Administrator's responsibilities (extreme vandalism and so forth), Jimmy Wales as the Benevolent Dictator can step in to guide the community back to a place in line with the Five Pillars. So, just as Wikipedia's Administrators and Benevolent Dictator function as servants of the Wikipedia community who help the Editors to effectively amass "the sum of all human knowledge," a congregation's elected leaders and pastor function to serve the congregation in effectively participating in the mission and ministry God has called each of them to.

Churches can stop being afraid they are going to miss out if they don't have *the right pastor* in their pulpit. One person is not going to make or break a community of faith. True, a good pastor will bring ideas that a congregation may not have thought of previously, but so will all the other members of the congregation. Pinning all of our hopes on finding that one person who will show us the right way to do things is a big mistake, so rather than spending time looking for that person, congregations should instead focus their energies on developing *wise groups*. As Surowiecki says, "The real key, it turns out, is not so much perfecting a particular method, but satisfying the conditions . . . that a group needs to be smart."[16]

In the following chapters, we will look at how these conditions can be and are already being satisfied in the context of gospel ministry. We will explore the ideas of diversity, independence of thought, and decentralization and how these conditions are being brought together for the benefit of the entire church. As we work our way through these four conditions, it will become increasingly clear that the open source church is already a reality. We simply need to know what we're looking for.

~ Chapter Three ~

Your Friendly Neighborhood Church Expert

I was not surprised to be asked the question. Given all I knew about First Presbyterian Church (FPC), it was sure to come. And it did.

By the time I met the Pastor Search Committee, FPC was a little more than 180 years old. Like most mainline churches, it had gone through the heyday of Christendom and for the past century had positioned itself as a real powerhouse in the community.

Forty years prior to my arrival, the congregation had experienced what was arguably the most prolific period of its life. A young pastor had been called who would stay for twenty years, and during that time many ministries in our community were started, literally in the middle of our sanctuary. The pastor's predilection for social justice found him marching in Selma, protesting the Vietnam War, helping to begin the Kansas City Chapter of PFLAG (Parents, Families, and Friends of Lesbians and Gays), co-organizing a community men's group of black and white members, inspiring and assisting the creation and development of a homeless transition ministry (whose model is now world renowned), and providing support for a few members to begin the Kansas City affiliate of Habitat for Humanity (the seventh to be organized worldwide). His preaching and passion were so well thought of that former students at the local Baptist college still tell me how they spent those four years "as a Presbyterian."

Subsequent pastors maintained and even grew the membership of the church, but a pastor who had such a broad impact on the community is a hard act to follow. For twenty years, the congregation had learned to operate in relation to his style. Changing course after a tenure like that was difficult for the membership.

Then there was the reality that the world was beginning to change in undeniable ways. Even though our little town just outside of Kansas City had always been slightly insulated from the drama of the city, people were beginning to recognize what a gem our community was, and many people began moving in to raise their families. This influx of new people brought new ideas and new expectations. Some of the long-time members of the church welcomed the change; some resisted.

New ideas about what it meant to be church reached our folks, and in the twenty-plus years between the era of social justice and my arrival, the congregation had struggled with its historic Presbyterian identity in both content (doctrine and ethics) and style. The worship wars came and went, and the congregation flirted with several strategies for being a seeker-sensitive church.

Those struggles resulted in a measure of disharmony that saw nearly all but the "I was born in this church" members leave. By the time I came on the scene, the church had been without a full-time, permanent pastor for more than three years. In fact, one older, long-time member confessed that at my installation as pastor, he wept through the majority of the service. "I was sure this church was going to die. I didn't think we'd ever find you."

And so I knew full well what question they would ask me: "What's your church growth plan?"

The Pastor as Expert

Although the question the search committee asked was, "What is your church growth plan?" what they were after was something much deeper. Something was amiss, and they knew it.

You didn't need to tell them that their community was different; they realized they didn't really know all their neighbors any more. You didn't need to tell them that the big Baptist church across the highway just kept getting bigger; they could watch it grow. You didn't need to explain to them how the Methodist church had done a better job of reaching out to families with youth; many of their kids had left FPC and had taken their grandchildren and gone there. They didn't want to give up the core identity they had as Presbyterians, but they clearly knew that what they were doing wasn't cutting the mustard.

Just like most congregations in the United States, the only way they knew to measure whether a church was successful was to count the number of people in the pews on a Sunday morning and the number of dollars in the offering plate. But the success of a church can be measured many different ways. If it's not church growth (and the accompanying dollars) it could be something else (for example, the number of people "saved," regardless of whether they become members). Their method of measuring success was not what caught my attention. What caught my attention was the word *your*.

"Pastor, what is *your* plan for growing our church? What is *your* idea about how we can attract more young families? What is *your* thought about contemporary worship?" (Interestingly, no one has yet asked me, "What's *your* budget plan for the church?")

Don't misunderstand me: I don't have anything against church growth. If a community is faithfully living its calling from God in the world, then people will notice and want to participate in that. If a church is faithful to Christ's mission, I believe some measure of growth can usually be expected. However, the issue I knew I would have to attend to with my new congregation, from day one, was their expectation that I was coming to be their resident "church expert."

It's not hard to see why. From where they sat, wasn't I the one who had just spent three years at a prestigious theological institution where I learned not only theology and biblical studies but also all manner of practical concepts? Wasn't I the one who had worked in campus ministry and as a student pastor in a church plant geared toward postmodern young adults? Wasn't I the one who had been ordained to work as the program director for a world-recognized interfaith organization? Wasn't I the *expert*?

Indeed, their expectations were not all that unique. Citing research done by Pulpit and Pew, a report produced by the Presbyterian Church (USA) sums up a congregation's expectation of their pastor nicely:

> The Bible describes a variety of forms of ministry leadership. *Evangelists* served a critical role as the early Christian church began to organize. In the Middle Ages, the pastor as *mediator of sacramental grace* became primary. The sixteenth and seventeenth century Protestant Reformation's principles of sola scriptura and the priesthood of all believers, among other things, elicited the pastor as *preacher* and pastor as *ethical guide* models. Around 1900 and with growing literacy new images and metaphors for pastoral ministry began to emerge, especially after the First World War. In no uniform order or pure forms, pastoral ministry models of *professional educator, psychologist/counselor, agent of social change,* and *manager of the church* surfaced as ideals. Recent research shows many congregants expect their pastor to master each of these models; *to be an expert in each of these roles* [final emphasis mine].[1]

Many churches are not sure how to navigate the waters of the changing postmodern landscape, and so they still rely on the model that they have used for years: find a really smart pastor, and pay her to do it for us.

Experts Are Overrated

In the modern West, particularly in the United States, we have been taken in by the cult of the expert. Our national imagination is densely populated with Lone Ranger and "pull yourself up by your own bootstraps" Horatio Alger types. We love iconoclasts who strike out on their own and do something remarkable. We celebrate individuality to the extreme. Because of this common mythos, we believe that ultragifted and intelligent *experts* are out there, and we are convinced that if we could just find them and convince them to help us, our troubles would be over.

This would be a remarkable solution if it were not for a couple of problems. First, when we are honest, we recognize that we don't have a firm grasp on the particular characteristics that identify one as an expert. Second, even if we *could* delineate a set of "expert" characteristics, we don't know what level of skill, giftedness, or intelligence someone would need to be worthy of the title *expert*.

Consider the relationship between natural ability and a learned skill set. Are we willing to call a woman with natural ability an expert even if she does not know the formal ways that her ability can or could be applied? If a man has very little natural ability in a given field or endeavor but spends an inordinate amount of time amassing technical knowledge on the subject and the skill to perform tasks satisfactorily, do we call him an expert?

I believe that we would be more comfortable calling the man an expert. To be sure, we would acknowledge that the woman is very gifted in her area, but we would hesitate to call her an expert because experts are supposed to be knowledgeable of their subjects inside and out. The woman may be the most gifted public speaker you have ever heard, but her inability to critically analyze a speech brings her well short of what we expect from an expert. The man, on the other hand, may give only an adequate speech, but we trust his intelligence and *expertise* when he demonstrates his skill at analysis.

When it comes to determining expertise, we tend to favor learned skill sets over natural ability. We do this because the capability to learn a skill set acts as a signal for us that this person or that will have the ability to amass skill in various areas. According to James Surowiecki, author of *The Wisdom of Crowds*, "We intuitively assume that intelligence is fungible, and that people who are excellent in one intellectual pursuit would be excellent in another. But that is not the case with experts. Instead, the fundamental truth about expertise is that it is, as [W. G.] Chase has said, 'spectacularly narrow.'"[2] Surowiecki goes on to note that no real evidence supports the idea that someone can be an expert of intangible disciplines such as decision making, policy, or strategy. Because the situations in which these disciplines are applied are so varied and complex, becoming an expert (if it were possible) would consume more than a lifetime of training. And yet, even after only three years of seminary training, aren't those precisely the kinds of things that congregations hope their pastors are experts in?

I believe the problem of expecting the pastor to be the all-knowing expert can be solved at the level of expectations, about what we *actually expect* our pastors to be and do. As we noted above, we want our pastors to be experts in practical matters like leading worship, education, pastoral care, administration, and community organizing. And yet, typically, decisions about whether the candidate is qualified to fulfill a congregation's expectations in these areas rest upon a very few number of conversations with a search committee, one sermon before the congregation, and parishioners' feelings about whether they connected to the candidate during the three to five minutes they talked to her at the "getting to know you" reception the day before in the chaotic fellowship hall.

This scenario doesn't bother us, however, because we assume (due to our belief in the fungibility of intelligence) that if the candidate can make a strong interpersonal connection, answer the search committee's questions to its satisfaction, and deliver a well-prepared sermon, then they must be "exactly the person we're looking for." Their interpersonal skills and successful delivery of a dynamite sermon translate, in our minds, to a perceived ability to excel in administrating the church's day-to-day activities and to effectively guide church boards and committees in carrying out the congregation's broader ministry. I think it is not far from the truth to say that congregations vote on a pastor based primarily on her preaching skills and then are shocked if she's not a great administrator.

Pastors, also, are aware of the disconnect between training and expectations. When pastors say things like "They didn't teach me this in seminary," what they are usually talking about are skills one would learn in business school. Yet they can't tell anyone that they are not equipped for the task, so, rather than find themselves without a job, I see pastors all over the country giving in to the expectation that they *can* be good administrators because they know this is what congregations want. I am not referring to those who are maliciously trying to fool people and take advantage of a situation but to those folks who, day to day, are put into positions where they just don't know what they are doing. But people are counting on them. What are they supposed to do? Imagine that you are a pastor in this situation: What would you do if an entire church were counting on you? Like most others, you would remind yourself that you can do this, and step up and try to meet expectations, wouldn't you? You would *not* admit you don't know what you're doing. In fact, you would continually tell yourself that you could until you believed it.

There's a psychological name for this tendency. It's called the "Dunning-Kruger effect," named for David Dunning and

Justin Kruger of Cornell University, which they established in their 1999 research paper "Unskilled and Unaware of It: How Difficulties in Recognizing One's Own Incompetence Lead to Inflated Self-Assessments."[3] Dunning and Kruger make several large claims in their paper regarding not just a person's competence but also one's inability to correctly assess his or her level of competence.

The pair conducted several tests across a range of areas (humor, logical reasoning, grammar) to first measure a person's level of competence. Then they took a further step and asked those tested to rate themselves in relation to the others who participated in the study. What they found was pretty amazing.

When they plotted participants' competence scores on a bell curve, they found the scores fell in an expected pattern: most folks in the middle and fewer at either end. Those who scored at the very top of the curve had a tendency to doubt their achievements. In the self-evaluation, they indicated (on average) they assumed they had fared better than three-quarters of their cohorts when, in fact, they had performed better than 90 percent of them. Conversely, those at the bottom end of the curve held an inflated opinion of their abilities. And when I say inflated, I mean *inflated*. In one test of logical reasoning, the bottom rung of participants indicated they believed they had outperformed 60 percent of their peers when in fact they had beaten out just 12 percent. A 48 percent difference! Not only did they lack the competence to score well on the test, they also didn't even know they scored poorly. Showing them the disparity did nothing to rectify the problem either. As Dunning and Kruger write, "Despite seeing the superior performance of their peers, bottom-quartile participants continued to hold to the mistaken impression that they had performed just fine."[4] A key finding from Dunning and Kruger's work can be summarized:

While the highly competent get doubtful, the incompetent get overconfident.

This point is important for this discussion because a direct correlation exists between people's inability to assess their own competence and their inability to assess the competence of others. For a given task, we are incapable of accurately determining who actually is or might be competent. Not only are those claiming to be experts probably not, but also most of us simply don't have the ability to pick them. As Surowiecki puts it in *The Wisdom of Crowds*, "And if a group is so unintelligent that it will flounder without the right expert, it's not clear why the group would be intelligent enough to recognize an expert when it found him." His underlying thesis that "chasing the expert is a mistake, and a costly one at that,"[5] advises us to stop hunting for an expert and ask the crowd for solutions instead, because it probably knows.

Congregations should quit trusting and expecting that pastors know everything about how to conduct the business of the church. A pastor's area of expertise is actually quite narrow. If we continue insisting that pastors be our resident church experts, we will find that our expectation causes more problems than it solves. If we continue trusting one person to expertly address all areas of church life, things will begin to fall apart. A better (and, I would argue, more faithful) plan of action is to begin tapping into the wisdom of the priesthood of all believers.

A Group of Normal People

When charged with assembling a group of leaders, the congregation's first impulse will more than likely be to explore how they can gather a group of people who are highly successful in the various ministries and administrative areas the church board is responsible for. Even though relying on one person is a bad idea, a group of people would naturally offset the downsides (the logic goes), especially if a congregation finds several highly successful individuals. This approach has two interrelated flaws not readily apparent.

First, this approach tempts us to continue our reliance on those we consider experts. Imagine a person in a congregation who is intelligent enough to have become a foreman in a construction company or a partner in an accounting firm. Let us say that this person finds himself elected to the congregation's governing board for the same reasons many congregational leaders are elected to their congregation's board: he has demonstrated some significant measure of success in his life. The thinking goes that because individuals have demonstrated success in their fields and have measurable and repeatable skill sets, they possess the needed qualities to sit on the congregation's board.

Chances are also good that these new board members will most certainly be tasked with overseeing property and finance, respectively. Buttressed by long-held expectations, the congregation tells itself that it would be a shame to see people of such intelligence and skill let their gifts go to waste. So, because they are the *experts*, the congregation simply turns over these responsibilities to them, and then it is back to square one. There is a chance that these new board members might also possess the skills and disposition to be a board member. I will return to this topic in the final chapter, but even if they do possess the necessary skills and disposition, the standard operating procedure of most church boards, which is informed by the expectations of most congregations, prevents boards from utilizing them. For now, it is sufficient to say that the expectations and procedures of most church boards turn congregational leaders into nothing more than glorified worker bees.

I believe a major reason for this situation is that, in the absence of a working understanding of what the church (at various levels) is and does, many congregations draw upon the one discipline in which they feel relatively comfortable and try to apply the principles they find there to the church. Again, fungibility comes into play as congregations all over repeat the line, "A church should behave like a business." I believe they assume the church can and should operate in this manner because they see almost every other area of their life taking its cues from the business sector. Why shouldn't our churches do the same?

In all fairness to the intentions of those faithful women and men who have said this, nonprofit organizations (such as the church) have learned and can learn much from our for-profit siblings. Good accounting and hiring practices are a must. Checks and balances are a necessity when it comes to money handling, and obtaining background checks on employees and volunteers is good and right. Yet, in spite of our reasons for taking cues from business, we in the church must be careful as we seek to survey popular business literature and try to make the church fit those practices.

Congregations are not businesses. Various gatherings of Christians have different understandings about what the purpose of the church is (at its various levels), but just as *Wikipedia* is clear that it is not a soapbox, newspaper, or repository for cutting-edge research, the church can and should be clear that it is not a business. Just as *Wikipedia* has made clear that it is an encyclopedia, the church must also make clear that it is the church.

When we unreflectively strive to apply business principles to the life of our congregations, we implicitly make the assumption that a congregation and a business have the same bottom line, or (at the least) one that can be treated similarly. The values of hospitality and celebrating difference are supplanted by efficiency and cohesiveness. We begin to make decisions about budget items based almost entirely on what will positively affect our cash flow. We treat our employees as widget makers, and compensation is based on associated productivity goals. (I know of one youth director who was fired because he did not grow the youth group by the number of kids the church board had projected he could.) As missional church thinker Reggie McNeal points out in his book *Missional Renaissance*, we gauge our success as a church by counting "how many, how often, how much"—how many people are involved, how often are they involved, and how much they give. McNeil says that, all too often, programmatic decisions are based not on the "personal development" of the people God has entrusted to our care but on how many people attend our functions.

Enter the congregation's highly successful new board members, who assume (backed by the expectations of their congregation) that the lessons they have learned in the business world are transferable to the church world, and the church finds itself back where it started: with experts in charge.

Another part of the problem with trying to recruit a group of experts is that we don't know how to define what, exactly, an expert is. Recalling the discussion of the Dunning-Kruger effect, we believe we have experts in our congregations, so we name certain people as such, despite not having the ability to actually identify them. How do we do this? We might admit that we don't have firm criteria to apply, but we will still claim to be able to identify them in same way that former United States Supreme Court Justice Potter Stewart spoke of being able to defining hard-core pornography: "I can't tell you what it is, but I know it when I see it." We don't know who the people are, but we know them when we see them. They are the people who are "smart enough to just get it." And while we may think that the more board members we have who resemble someone who *gets it* the better off we will be, in fact we would actually be quite mistaken.

Imagine a group is assembled in which all the members possess to a large degree what we have unconsciously defined as intelligence (using intelligence as the criterion to determine whether they *get it*). If such criteria were to be used, what we would begin to realize is that all the group members would more than likely resemble one another. They would have similar worldviews and opinions about various situations. Their life experiences would look remarkably similar. They would have similar backgrounds, for they would probably inhabit the same social class if not the same race and gender. They would all have close to the same level of education. In short, there wouldn't be much significant difference between them at all.

The reason this group's members would closely resemble one another largely has to do with the ways in which people assess and rank desirable characteristics. As an example, let's take a look at *New Yorker* columnist and bestselling author Malcolm Gladwell's discussion of the psychological principle known as the "Flynn effect" (named for the social scientist James Flynn), which states that as long as IQ tests have been administered, the raw scores of IQ tests have increased by three points per decade.

> If an American born in the nineteen-thirties has an I.Q. of 100, the Flynn effect says that his children will have I.Q.s of 108, and his grandchildren I.Q.s of close to 120—more than a standard deviation higher. If we work in the opposite direction, the typical teen-ager of today, with an I.Q. of 100, would have had grandparents with average I.Q.s of 82—seemingly below the threshold necessary to graduate from high school. And, if we go back even farther, the Flynn effect puts the average I.Q.s of the schoolchildren of 1900 at around 70, which is to suggest, bizarrely, that a century ago the United States was populated largely by people who today would be considered mentally retarded.[6]

Flynn is anything but an IQ fundamentalist and has spent a good portion of his career challenging the ways in which intelligence is assessed. He says that the shifts in intelligence test scores should give us a "crisis of confidence." In trying to reason why the shift itself happens, he surmises that either children these days are much smarter than their parents and grandparents or the methods used to assess intelligence are themselves flawed.

Flynn points out that the main reason IQs rise is actually due to a specific category of IQ tests— "similarities." In this category, respondents are asked questions such as, "In what way are 'dogs' and 'rabbits' alike?" The *correct* answer is, of course, that they are both mammals. But Gladwell observes that if you were to ask a nineteenth-century American this question, the answer you would likely receive is, "You use dogs to hunt rabbits." Isn't that also a *correct* answer?

> If the everyday world is your cognitive home, it is not natural to detach abstractions and logic and the hypothetical from their concrete referents," Flynn writes. Our great-grandparents may have been perfectly intelligent. But they would have done poorly on I.Q. tests because they did not participate in the twentieth century's great cognitive revolution, in which we learned to sort experience according to a new set of abstract categories. In Flynn's phrase, we have now had to put on "scientific spectacles," which enable us to make sense of the WISC [Wechsler Intelligence Scale for Children, one of the most widely used IQ tests] questions about similarities. To say that Dutch I.Q. scores rose substantially between 1952 and 1982 was another way of saying that the Netherlands in 1982 was, in at least certain respects, much more cognitively demanding than the Netherlands in 1952. An I.Q., in other words, measures not so much how smart we are as how *modern* we are.[7]

Gladwell goes on to remind us that at several points in United States' history, various immigrant groups were thought to have a much lower intelligence than their already assimilated American neighbors, which we can now generally attribute to their ignorance of the rules of the modern Western game. Once these groups were assimilated to a certain point, their IQs rose dramatically.

Even though Flynn's distrust of IQ tests concerns a *formal* method of assessing intelligence (and, therefore, preparedness), I believe the core of that distrust applies all the more to *informal* methods. Just as IQ is actually measuring how modern a person is (do they know the rules about how to succeed in a modern world?), a congregation's process of selecting its leaders is actually measuring how well a person knows the "unwritten rulebook" Carol Howard Merritt talks about. At their most basic, both methods are actually assessing who knows the rules.

The average size of a Presbyterian church is between 100 and 125 members, translating to 75 to 90 people who consistently participate in some church gathering (worship, Sunday school, committee work). The nominating committee for churches of this size will have five to seven members. Assuming that the majority of those 75 to 90 active members are eligible to serve in formal congregational leadership, it is safe to say that no matter whose name comes up for discussion when considering candidates, someone on the nominating committee is going to know them rather well.

As I have sat in nominating committee meetings, I have noticed a real hesitancy on the committee's part to talk plainly about their neighbors. According to my denomination's constitution, the committee is to nominate people "of strong faith, dedicated discipleship, and a love of Jesus Christ as Savior and Lord," whose life should be "a demonstration of the Christian gospel in the church and in the world."[8] Still, members feel very uncomfortable with what they interpret as passing judgment on another person's faith and character, especially someone they know well. Rather than have conversations about character and faith that feel like they are tattling on their friends, these committees resort to general discussions about a person's successes in their vocational life and their history with the church. At all levels of the church, I can't recall a discussion about whether a candidate has demonstrated willingness toward self-sacrifice or a commitment to evangelization (what I would consider to be two essential aspects of demonstrating the Christian gospel). But I have heard many conversations that begin by highlighting the fact that a candidate has served on several committees

of the church. Most of these comments are meant to be a statement about the candidate's commitment to the congregation,
but I often hear some variation of "She already knows how we
do things." As with an IQ test, the ones rewarded (in this case,
elected to the church board) are the ones who already know the
rules of the particular game being played.

Educator and author Ruby K. Payne makes a statement
about the different rules systems in her book *A Framework for
Understanding Poverty*. Payne's thesis is that the various socioeconomic groups we each inhabit have "hidden rules," systems
of communication and values that make it virtually impossible
for us to interact with others. The ways in which members of
the middle class communicate, and what it is they value, appear
to a member of the lower class like the language and values of
a foreign country. In fact, Payne contends, if someone wants to
elevate her social standing (from lower to middle class, or from
middle to upper class) she must be willing to forgo her previous
system of communication and live by the "hidden rules" of her
new class group. People tend to gravitate toward and reward
those whom we deem are like us. Most of us also assume that
if someone speaks the same way we do—if they emphasize
similar points, employ similar ideas and metaphors, use turns
of phrase that we might ourselves use—then they must possess
some measure of what we think of as intelligence.

I have repeatedly seen the effects of this in groups I have
worked with. There usually seem to be at least two unofficial
factions, and it probably won't surprise you to learn that they
usually form along class lines. These two groups value different
things, communicate differently (a la Payne's "hidden rules"),
and rarely see eye to eye on anything. On a couple of occasions,
when I have been responsible for leading such a group, I have
had what I refer to as the "those people" discussion. No one
is mean or offensive (quite the contrary). But they usually say
something about the group being able to be more effective if

so-and-so were not a part of the process. "He just doesn't get it. He keeps raising issues that are not important and asking questions that don't have anything to do with anything. We need to get him shaped up, or we need to find someone else." Just as IQ tests measure not a level of intelligence but conformity to modernity, *those people* are being judged by whether their ability to "get it" measures up to the notions of someone in a another socioeconomic class. (Typically these accusations come from members of higher classes, but we shouldn't rule out the reverse happening.)

A Collective Expert

The net result of an unreflective method of choosing our group of experts—a *collective expert*, if you will—is that we have created a group of very similar people who are destined for failure. The more homogeneity a group has, the less chance it has of making intelligent, beneficial decisions. *A collective expert is just as overrated as an individual one.*

Regardless of the group's defining characteristics, when group members are similar, they tend to become cohesive fairly quickly. This cohesiveness is deceptive. We interpret the cohesiveness as a good thing because it seemingly allows us to get our work done more effectively and efficiently. But the actual effect of cohesion is that it promotes reliance upon the group to such a degree that members become insulated from outside opinions.

Once cohesion has been firmly established, group members are now subject to the logic of the group. Each member assumes the group is right when assessing key questions ("If everyone sees it this way, it must be right, right?"), and any counteropinion or caution is dismissed as out of touch and unhelpful to the process (at best) or as combative and detrimental (at worst). Psychologist Irving Janis referred to this phenomenon as *groupthink*: "a type of thought within a deeply cohesive in-group whose members try to minimize conflict and reach consensus without critically testing, analyzing, or evaluating ideas."[9] Since everyone in the group shares a startling number of characteristics, there is almost no chance of them becoming aware of their biases regarding what information is or is not important. Potentially key information is not received into the group's process, and the result is a less than stellar answer to whatever question is posed.

"But," you may ask, "are you saying that we could gather together a bunch of morons, and we'll be fine?" Well . . . kind of.

There is, to be sure, a certain level of knowledge that one must possess to be a functional member of any group. When, for example, the congregation I serve elects a new slate of elders to serve a term, they must be instructed on the basics of the Presbyterian system of government and the policies and procedures of our congregation's administration methods, and they must be functionally acquainted with the doctrinal confessions of our church (which they have each vowed to be guided by).

But, truly, that is really all they need to know. There have been a couple of years when, for some reason, I did not get a chance to sit down with the new elders and give them this training. Although they still contributed to the group's process, their lack of preparation left them at a disadvantage because they felt ill-equipped to participate. I am sure you could guess the result. They tended to defer to the *experts*, who "obviously knew what they were doing." Yet, beyond the knowledge needed for basic functioning, a group of normal people can make great decisions every time.

It Takes All Kinds of People to Make the World Go Round

So what is *normal?* The answer, of course, is that *normal* is whatever you think it is and whatever I think it is. We each judge reality based on our own experience and uses it as a point of comparison for everything we encounter. We are each normal.

Yet, when we assume that our normal is or should be what normal is for everyone else, our ability to read our context is thrown into jeopardy. Don Browning, author of *A Fundamental Practical Theology*, argues that we need to remember to consider a question like "How do we understand this concrete situation in which we must act?" as a deeply theological task. If we believe that God is at work in the world, then being able to describe accurately what we understand God to be doing is of utmost importance if we are to know where to join God's work.

This place we're talking about—God's world—is full of nooks and crannies. There is no way you and I could ever accurately describe it all. There is no way you and I could ever know all of what God is up to in this world, even though you and I are very different kinds of people, even though you and I do not know each other and have the most divergent set of interests imaginable. Even as different as you and I are, we will not even begin to approach a comprehensive understanding of God and God's work. But we will do better than if we were the same.

Even though only you and I are describing God's world, being very different people is actually an advantage. Each of us sees things that the other does not. If we are riding in a car together, you can look out one window and I can look out another, and between the two of us we can describe twice as much landscape. This is actually one of the most basic reasons not to rely on an expert—because no matter how expert a person really is, he or she is still just one person.

Being able to describe the landscape of any place, tangible or intangible, is the first step toward fulfilling a purpose. Whether you are crossing a mountain range or serving those in need in your community, knowing what kind of terrain you are about to traverse informs every decision you make about your journey. When churches populate their governing boards with people who are simply carbon copies of one another, they have severely limited their ability to describe the landscape in which they are being called to do ministry. If the various levels of a church are going to effectively pursue the mission of God, members of the body must attend to diversity.

When it comes right down to it, diversity is not something that we as Christians attend to because it's the nice thing to do. We don't seek it out because it's politically correct. We don't—or shouldn't—concern ourselves with it because we feel compelled. We don't do it simply because we think Jesus told us to—because our reading of the Scriptures begs for diversity in the church.

No, the reason Christians attend to the ideal of diversity is that it is a necessary component in achieving the work that God has created, called, and gathered us together to accomplish. We *do* diversity because we will fail in our calling from God if we do not. When we do not attend to diversity (in as many forms of it as we can conceive), we make vital mistakes in our ministry and mission, because the composition of our groups allows us to be insular and self-referential. Diversity is who we are as the body of Christ. We are not all "hands" nor "feet," Paul reminds us. We are each unique, and it is the variety of our uniquenesses that allows us to pursue the calling God has given the church.

The old saying goes that if horses had gods, they would look like horses. We humans create things in our own images because that is what we know best. If those charged with caring for the church building are all able-bodied young men, the chances of them being attuned to the fact that the sanctuary is not handicap accessible is slim. If the worship committee is completely populated by women and men who revere the worship styles and habits they knew when they were children, then the worshiping life of that community will continue to resemble those memories. If the only people who sit on the Christian education committee are parents of young children, then the learning needs of older adults stand a good chance of being neglected.

It doesn't take an expert to remind us that what we each actually know and are aware of is relatively narrow, so when someone is charged with a task, they are going to draw on the resources they have to accomplish goals that sound reasonable to them. We will naturally do things that make sense to us, even if the reach of those things is not as broad as it needs to be. So, when we in the church are charged with gathering a group of "normal" people, the most effective thing we can do is to focus on ensuring that there is as much diversity around the table as possible.

You might be saying to yourself, "That's great, but my church is mostly _____ (insert demographic group here). How am I supposed to pull together a diverse group?" Never fear. You don't have to import folks from the big cities. Even just one person who is different from everyone else makes a group smarter. One elder serving our congregation constantly tells me that she doesn't think she's that smart, but she knows how to ask a really good question. And she does. She asks a lot of questions. I have seen time and again that simply because she won't automatically go along with the movement of the group, she makes the group smarter. She asks several probing questions, sometimes on every piece of business before the group. She keeps people on their toes and ensures that they are attentive to all the possibilities in a given action because they have no idea what questions they will be asked about it.

The more perspectives a group has, the better. Making sure that it represents a broad spectrum of beliefs and opinions—right and left, modern and traditional—means that many theological convictions will be taken into account. The more diverse a group is theologically, the less chance it has of being either irrelevant or heretical—or both.

The more diverse a group's life experience, the better. For example, as one who has never served in the military, I am going to have a particular perspective on armed conflict that is quite different from the faithful man who served in World War II and witnessed atrocities that still keep him up at night. When we begin discussing the ethics involved in armed conflict, he is going to be able to offer a perspective that I cannot. While war is an abstract concept to me, it is very real to him.

The easiest way to ensure diversity is to make sure that our groups are representative in race, gender, class, and education. The hourly wage earner will bring a perspective on life different from the salaried corporate vice president. Those with postcollege education are going to see the world differently from those who may not have graduated high school. And it is no surprise any longer to see that women and men, and different racial or ethnic groups, encounter the world in vastly different ways, often in ways that someone of a different group cannot comprehend until they stare the person right in the face (and often not even then!).

This point was brought home to me recently when I met, for the first time in real life, my Twitter friend Margaret Aymer. Margaret is a brilliant woman who teaches New Testament at the Interdenominational Theological Center in Atlanta. She and I had been friends online for about a year. We both love good food and the joy of teaching, and we are both committed to open source technologies. I had seen her picture only online and assumed that she is an African American woman. I knew that her husband is a French man, but I didn't think anything of it. In light of all I thought I knew about her (a black woman teaching at a historically black denominational school, with some worldly interests), I found her project of interpreting the Bible as an immigrant narrative to be nothing more than a highly interesting abstract thought experiment.

Then I met her and learned she was born in Barbados and lived much of her life in Jamaica and Antigua before immigrating to the United States.

My entire understanding of Margaret was blown open. Things about her that had confused me were brought into very clear focus, just because I knew that one piece of information about her. For her, immigrant status is *real*. She's not playing with the idea; she *lives* the idea. She shared that she always has to deal with the fact that most folks think of her as *a black woman* and with their preconceptions and biases about that identity. But for her, her status as an immigrant allows her a perspective that I had never heard before, and (closer to our point) her racial and ethnic identity and political status as an immigrant sheds light on the biblical text in way I had never encountered. Margaret helps us all accomplish the mission of God, because she brings her whole self to her work.

The benefit of diversity is this: When *different* is *normal*, everyone is able to bring their whole selves to bear on the present issue, problem, or question. When no one particular characteristic is a majority, everyone is able to offer the particular gifts God has given them. As we will see in the next chapter, ensuring that people feel free to contribute the unique gifts they possess makes the crowd wiser, and being wise can't happen without diversity.

It's *Your* Church

So what did I say in answer to the Pastor Search Committee's question, "What's *your* church growth plan?"

"I don't have one," I said. "All I have is a 'Be Faithful to Jesus Plan,' which would include *helping you all* figure out how to spread Christ's grace and peace in this community. If I become your pastor, I'll be with you for only a season. But this community is where God has called you to be the body of Christ. This is *your* church, and you all know your town better than I do. There's no way I could suggest something better than the ideas already present in your congregation."

Congregations need to stop thinking they need an expert to solve their problems, for everything they need is already present in the diverse people God has gathered together in each community. Once we recognize that fact, our next step is ensuring that each person can bring his or her whole self to the table.

Chapter Four

So If Everyone Else Jumped Off the Bridge, Would You?

The first job I took right out of seminary was as the program director of an interfaith organization. One of my responsibilities, naturally, was to provide staff assistance to a few of the board's committees. We had some pretty great people on our board—movers and shakers in their respective work worlds and some folks who were highly involved in the life of their various religious communities.

For a while, I did my best to be a resource to them, to offer them the information they needed and to help them reflect on the tasks they had at hand. But they never got anything done. At times, my job was like slogging through thick mud. I wasn't sure what was going on. These were intelligent and passionate people who got things done in their own communities of faith, and they very much cared about interfaith cooperation. I soon discovered that, while they knew how to move and operate within their own communities, several confessed that they felt in over their heads when it came to figuring out how to encourage the various communities to work together.

One day someone came to me with some advice: "One thing you need to remember, Landon, is that this is a hobby for most of these people. And while it is a hobby for them, this is your job."

Even though I knew I needed to heed that advice to get things done and keep my job, something about it felt off to me. The committees were the picture of diversity. They included women and men from several different religious communities and multiple racial and ethnic backgrounds. Many of the committee members were well educated, but not all of them. By all accounts, this should have been a highly productive and wise crowd. Instead, everyone deferred to me. Because this organization was their "hobby," as opposed to my "job," they felt inadequate to the task. It was never lost on me that avenues for action I suggested were often the ones finally adopted. I certainly tried to do thorough research and preliminary thinking in order to provide them with solid rationales for my suggestions, but I could never quite shake the feeling that we left a lot of gold buried in our small patch of land simply because everyone thought we should dig where I had suggested.

Sometimes a complementary force also came into play. At times someone actually *would* have an idea about what to do, but they didn't want to rock the boat. I or a member of the committee would give an analysis of a problem, laying out whatever issue was facing us as well as the variables we felt needed to be taken into account, and then we would open the item up for conversation. But no one spoke. We heard a few cursory offerings of thanks for the good presentation, but, even in the silence, I had the sense that there was some passion around the table. The trouble was that no one wanted to go first. No one wanted to be that person.

Finally, someone would speak, usually giving a well-reasoned argument for taking a particular course of action. The pros and cons would be discussed, and the group would rarely end up doing anything other than the original suggestion made. Now, that might not seem too bad to you, but sitting in that meeting, watching the body language of people I knew fairly well, I could see there was a problem. Often two or three other people were waiting for an opportunity to offer their ideas. However, once they saw that the conversation was taking a particular course, they seemed to weigh the value of offering their alternative idea, eventually deciding not to, so that they would not cause the group more work.

Parliamentarians will not be so bothered by this outcome. In systems of ordered debate, everyone present is free to offer their perspective on the item at hand by amending it or suggesting an alternate course of action. And while I will agree that these systems do have their place, I believe that the dynamics of small groups of religious people often don't lend themselves too well to systems like Robert's Rules of Order. What I saw in those meetings (which I have also seen in countless church meetings, something which I am sure happens in congregations all over) was people either doubting the distinctiveness and viability of their ideas compared with the one presented or afraid of offending one another. It doesn't matter that I have the right to amend an idea or suggest an alternative course of action if I think that Mary is much smarter than I am and has a better idea, or if I am acutely aware that Joe has a pretty fragile ego about ideas he has worked hard on.

When it comes right down to it, most of us are going to give in to the wills and wishes of others on a regular basis, because we believe that "going along to get along" is a good idea, particularly when we would be going along with someone we think is smarter than we are.

It's Who We Are

Our tendency to "go along to get along" is really not our fault. Most of us have been taught that consensus and conformity are the values good people of faith are supposed to pursue. But I believe that, especially for Christians, this way of being is deeply woven into the very fabric of our self-identity.

In a plain reading of the scriptural text, consensus and conformity seem to be promoted throughout the Bible, especially in the letters of the New Testament. We are encouraged to present a unified front to the rest of the world. People should not see us arguing and fighting. They should not see us at odds with one another. We are also encouraged to stick to the tried and true—to be conservative (in the truest sense of the word) in our approach to the Christian life. To be sure, each of the passages of Scripture in which we find these admonitions offers us a deep understanding of the ways in which a Christian will behave, but they are clouded by a couple of pervading realities.

First, most of us never even scratch beyond the surface of these passages to probe a historical reading of the text. We don't ask how the first listeners and readers would have understood the concepts presented or the possible translations of the key words that inform those concepts. We assume that our modern Western views on life are equivalent to the view that those in the biblical community would have had. Second, preachers have a hard job selling self-sacrifice to a people who are told almost every other day of the week by corporate advertisements that they deserve to have the things they want to have. Rather than dig into the deep truths of the Bible, many preachers choose not to rock the boat, and so they boil the biblical text down to a simple admonition: "Be nice, and rely on the tried and true." That, friends, is a recipe for disaster.

Because we consistently hear messages advocating consensus and conformity, we assume that when we see those things present in our group proceedings, we are seeing evidence of the work of the Holy Spirit bringing us together. We assume that the cohesion we spoke of in the last chapter is an example of the unity of the people of God. But what we often think of as a movement of the Holy Spirit is, in fact, not.

Theologically speaking, in creed and confession after creed and confession, the Holy Spirit is always spoken of in relation to the *whole* church. The Holy Spirit is the gift of God's very self to the church to be the power of the church. And yet, in what we think of as Spirit-filled moments, we are often actually witnessing the power of one person to sway a group, not the actions of the group itself.

I think you and I can and should be gracious enough to acknowledge that these people are not usually manipulating the group intentionally, but we would be fools to say that it does not happen. We all know people who are unafraid to speak their minds regardless of the issue (you might be one of them), and because they speak their minds with boldness and conviction, everyone thinks that's the way to go. Regardless of the information that each group member has, they decide instead to follow the lead of the people before them because they believe that those people must have better information. Far from being a movement of the Holy Spirit, however, this pattern or behavior is what learning theorists refer to as an *information cascade*.

Joel Osteen and Hot Pockets

A few years ago, pastor and author Nadia Bolz-Weber decided to watch Christian television for twenty-four hours straight and write about it. Bolz-Weber is the pastor of a Lutheran church plant in Denver called House for All Sinners and Saints, an emergent faith community of urban folks who "don't have any desire to live near an Applebee's."[1] The result of her daylong experiment is the book *Salvation on the Small Screen? 24 Hours of Christian Television.*

A little more than halfway through her challenge, Bolz-Weber encountered Joel Osteen, pastor of Lakewood Church in Houston, Texas. Lakewood is the largest congregation in the United States, with an average weekly attendance of 43,500. They meet in the former Compaq Center, where 16,800 people can worship at one time. Obviously, a lot of people like Joel Osteen.

Many people question the theological message Osteen is preaching, but whenever we do, the rebuttal is consistent: "God must be blessing him. He must be doing something right, or that many people wouldn't flock to his ministry." The assumption is that 43,500 people can't be wrong. Is that the case? Does it hold that the more popular something is, the better it is?

Bolz-Weber didn't think so. "There are times when the popularity of Joel Osteen is very confusing to me. But then I realize: there are times when the popularity of Hot Pockets is also confusing to me, so I choose not to dwell on it."[2] Regardless of the perceived level of importance of both Osteen and Hot Pockets, Bolz-Weber concluded that many people decide they like something for reasons that are often times far from rational. Is she saying that no one actually resonates with the message that Osteen is preaching? She is not. What she is intimating, however, is that the vast majority of those who are flocking to Lakewood Church are there not out of a conviction regarding the message but because they think something important must be happening and they don't want to miss out on it.

What Bolz-Weber is naming is actually a well-known principle in social psychology called *social proofing* (the belief that more people taking part in a particular action proves its importance), and it helps explain what we see in an information cascade. The most well-known experiment to demonstrate social proofing was conducted by Stanley Milgram, Leonard Bickman, and Lawrence Berkowitz in 1968. In their study, Milgram, Bickman, and Berkowitz planted an individual on a street corner to stare up at a tall building. They then counted the number of people who mimicked the plant's action. They ran the test several times, each time using more initial plants than the time before. They discovered that when only one person was staring up at the building, only 20 percent of passersby joined in the staring. However, when as few as five people were initially on the street corner, the number of compliant passersby jumped to 80 percent.

The unwitting participants in the experiment each thought to themselves, "If those five people are staring at something up there, then there must be something up there worth staring at." The experiment suggests that each additional person who participates in a behavior further validates the significance of the behavior. As James Surowiecki reflects, "The governing assumption seems to be that when things are uncertain, the best thing to do is just follow along."[3] Is the prosperity gospel that Osteen is preaching good and helpful? I'm not sure, so I'd better follow along just to be safe. Are Hot Pockets really worth my money? A lot of people eat them, so they must be. (I, however, think this suggests the need for mass psychological intervention.)

The tendency to follow along can be a good idea. As Surowiecki argues, groups often know what's best. It makes sense to follow their lead. But problems arise when too many people stop *contributing* to the group and start *relying* on the group. Surowiecki explains, "Errors in individual judgment won't wreck the group's collective judgment as long as those errors aren't systematically pointing in the same direction. One of the quickest ways to make people's judgments systematically biased is to make them dependent on each other for information."[4] He is encouraging us to not worry about members of the group having incomplete or incorrect information. The group will naturally counterbalance those errors. However, if people are depending on the person next to them for information, no one is left to correct the initial mistake. The appeal of Osteen is that he has so many followers. People pick up and move to Houston based on the testimony of someone else, which was based on the testimony of someone else, which was based on . . .

The antidote for this kind of systematic bias is to encourage group members to use *private information*, any data that only they possess. This information can include not only concrete facts but also opinions, beliefs, or personal intuition and interpretation. Think back to our *Millionaire* crowds. Each person in that studio used different private information to answer the question presented them. The aggregation of their individual answers, not some great in-studio compromise (and certainly not one answer based on what the lady in seat J-68 said), produced a wise result.

Because many church board members believe that out there is an expert who knows best what to do and are, therefore, already prone to self-doubt, when another board member is bold in his opinion about which direction to take, the others will naturally go along with him. The Milgram experiment suggests that as more people fall to the pressure exerted by the first person, the more likely it is the rest of the group will assume that person's suggestion is the best one.

This "falling in line" is at the heart of an information cascade. If a board member has private data that suggests an alternative course of action, she will immediately weigh whether that information is worth offering, because doing so will likely cause more work for the group. Consensus *is* the ultimate value, after all. Rather than rock the boat unnecessarily, individuals will fall in line with the group. "Everyone thinks that people are making decisions based on what [private data] they know when in fact people are making decisions based on what they think the people who came before them knew."[5] Too often, as they sit in church board meetings, members say either to themselves or aloud, "I'm happy to do whatever the group wants." Sometimes this decision is the result of pure indifference, but more often it comes from a lack of confidence, which opens the door to an information cascade.

So, If Everyone Else Jumped Off a Bridge . . .

However, not all unanimous group decisions are the result of unwittingly succumbing to a psychological principle. Christians are not that ridiculous. A significant reason we in the church make the decisions we do is that we desire to be faithful to this thing we have been entrusted with. We want to make good decisions!

Everyone who accepts a call to serve a congregation tries to live up to the expectation that their decisions will be in the best interests of the people they serve. Regardless of the polity (system of government) of a particular congregation, and even though leaders understand they are ultimately answerable only to God, they must also recognize that they serve a congregation of people who have trusted them to make good choices with the collective gifts of the community. These gifts may be financial or they may be the willingness of members to volunteer their time and skills. Whatever they are, they need to be used well. Good stewardship is explicit in a leader's call to serve the church.

Good stewardship means that our leaders should make sound choices about resources. What are we putting our finances toward, and does that reflect our understanding of who we are as the people of God in this place? What kinds of programs, activities, and events are we planning? Are we effectively using the gifts, skills, and time of those who have agreed to join in the church's work? Even though leaders in the Presbyterian Church (USA) are not technically answerable to congregation members (our elders do not vote as a reflection of the desires of "constituents"), if they consistently make choices that run counter to the implied agreement about who the congregation is, not only will they hear about it but also many members might leave and seek spiritual fellowship elsewhere.

However, fulfilling a congregation's expectations *can* become simply a response to fear and anxiety, avoiding any kind of innovative decision for fear of the congregational reaction. To paraphrase my favorite theologian, Paul Tillich, "Where fear and anxiety are present, sin is sure to follow." We make stupid decisions when we are afraid and anxious. Decisions informed by fear and anxiety are self-protective and reactionary.

And so, faced with change, too many churches retreat. To echo our earlier conversation, they do not know what to do with the changing theological and cultural landscape. They have perfected their ways of doing business over the course of generations, and they are hard pressed to do things any differently. When chaos comes a-calling, their first reaction is to become more conservative with the gifts at their disposal. Their uncertainty about the most effective ways to address these changes forces them to rely on tried and true methods that have served them well for years.

They often come by this behavior honestly. Perhaps, in their attempt to find that one pastor who could lead them through this vast cultural wilderness, they were burned. As Surowiecki says, "Chasing the expert is a mistake and costly one at that."[6] Perhaps they learned that lesson the hard way and are determined to not go down that road again.

I wonder how many traditional churches, during the worship wars, found themselves coerced or shamed into beginning a contemporary worship service? How many thousands of dollars did they spend to buy new sound equipment and install projectors and screens in their sanctuaries? How many beautiful buildings were ruined, in some people's minds, because of these technological "advances"? How deep did the congregation go, trusting in the "If you build it, they will come" mentality, only to find that no one came? You should have a hard time faulting these folks for wanting to avoid that kind of risky behavior again.

And yet, that lack of risk is killing them.

When those churches came out on the other side of their particular worship war, chances are good that the only folks still attending worship were those who had been members of that congregation for decades—those for whom the established tradition was comfortable. And yet, more than simple comfort drove them to established tradition. It was, in many cases, a firm belief that this way of connecting to God was the best. Given their understanding of who God is and what God intends through worship, the common belief and conviction was that those aims could best be accomplished through worship habits long established.

Before I go on, I want to be clear that this is just one example. Examples of the limiting perspectives of contemporary worship proponents could also be cited. I have been in worship planning sessions where anything that even hinted of "traditional" was cast aside with disdain. This tendency can be found in our understandings of Christian education, mission, and evangelism. The point here is not to beat up on the straw man of traditional worship but to help us to see that, in these moments, if we look honestly at those present, something striking becomes clear: *those in positions of influence are remarkably homogeneous.*

To some extent, this is a natural occurrence. As society has become more mobile, the phenomenon of the neighborhood parish has all but gone away. No longer do people have to be members of a particular congregation simply because there are no other options. It is now commonplace for people to drive several miles to attend worship at a church that they find more enjoyable. High church? Low church? Conservative? Liberal? It doesn't matter what your preferences are; most of us will be able to find a church that we feel matches us fairly close. As we learned in the previous chapter, Christian birds of a feather do flock together.

However, radical innovation is going to be extremely rare if it violates a congregation's self-understanding. When almost everyone present (and certainly the people of influence) all see things *the same way*, no one is going to be able to recognize the new thing that God is doing in their midst. The writer of the Proverbs communicates this way: "Where there is no vision, the people perish" (Prov. 29:18a KJV).

And yet, it is precisely in these environments where everyone sees things the same way that congregational leaders are trying to lead. Picking up the worship discussion again, I point to legendary church consultant Bill Easum, who claims that the number one way to jumpstart a "stuck church" into vital ministry in its community is to begin a worship service that more accurately reflects those you hope to reach with the gospel (which usually isn't a traditional worship service). The conventional wisdom of that congregation says, "We don't do that." The reason why is the key: "We tried that once and it failed."

Relying on conventional wisdom, ultimately, is not based in a desire for success, but in an aversion to risk. People participate in the information cascade and contribute to the social proof because we are afraid of striking out and perhaps making the wrong call. As Surowiecki helpfully points out, "Sticking with the [self-protective] crowd and failing small, rather than trying to innovate and run the risk of failing big, makes not just emotional sense but also professional sense."[7] If we fail by going small, we can at least point out that we were simply doing what everyone else was doing or would have done. We are not to blame; we were following the conventional wisdom. It is also easier to fail small. If we were to risk big and fail big, we would never hear the end of it. In fact, we might be so beat up that we would seriously consider leaving our church for another or leaving the church altogether.

However, there is hope for leaders in this situation. A good example of that hope is the advice the apostle Paul gives to his young colleague Timothy.

Power, Love, and Self-Discipline

Second Timothy is called one of the Pastoral Letters because it, 1 Timothy, and Titus convey pastor-to-pastor advice about pastoral issues. Don't let the English word *pastor* fool you. We're not talking about the modern job title but the ancient function played by congregational leaders. Their title meaning "shepherd," pastors are those in a congregation whose responsibility it is to ensure the safety and well-being of the membership so that they may do what God has called them to do.

Very early in the letter we find an interesting piece of encouragement from Paul to Timothy, a young man whom Paul met on one of his missionary journeys. He was a convert to the gospel of Jesus and became a close associate and emissary of Paul.

> I am grateful to God—whom I worship with a clear conscience, as my ancestors did—when I remember you constantly in my prayers night and day. Recalling your tears, I long to see you so that I may be filled with joy. I am reminded of your sincere faith, a faith that lived first in your grandmother Lois and your mother Eunice and now, I am sure, lives in you. For this reason I remind you to rekindle the gift of God that is within you through the laying on of my hands; for God did not give us a spirit of cowardice, but rather a spirit of power and of love and of self-discipline.
>
> —2 Tim. 1:3–7

Little is known about the writing of this letter. In fact, most scholars think that, rather than being an actual letter written by Paul, it was written much later "as if by Paul" in order for the church to address some pressing issues. One can only speculate as to the specifics of those issues, but the text as it is gives us some interesting clues.

Paul begins his letter by addressing a problem with Timothy that has produced "tears" and "cowardice" in him. Paul reminds his young friend of the "sincere faith" that he has had, a faith passed down to him from his grandmother and mother (whom he references by name!). What could have happened to cause Timothy—one so strong in the faith that he was sent as Paul's personal ambassador—to retreat in fear and tears?

The only guess I hazard is based on a verse in Paul's first letter to Timothy. In the midst of a list of instructions about what to teach the community he has been sent to serve, Paul tells Timothy to "let no one despise your youth, but set the believers an example in speech and conduct, in love, in faith, in purity" (1 Tim. 4:12). Do not let them look down on you because you are young, Paul says. You have gifts from God for ministry, and do not let someone tell you that you do not simply because of your age. They may have an opinion about your abilities or maturity, but all you can do is set an example for them. Grow a thick skin, he's saying. You can't let them get to you.

I think they got to him.

Being a congregational leader is hard. Discerning where God might be calling this group of people at this time is difficult. I am reminded again that in *Wikipedia*, the community leaders call themselves the janitors. That's what a lot of us feel like sometimes. The work is thankless, people resist right and left, and we are the ones who are left to clean up the messes. It should not be surprising that the burnout rate for clergy is so high and that most congregational leaders want nothing more to do with serving the church after their terms have ended. They are almost always exhausted and usually bitter by the end. Let's be honest: it's easier to just give in, to go along to get along, and to replicate the same programs and experiences that the congregation has always had.

Many pastors and church board members have returned from meetings saying things like, "Who needs enemies with friends like these?" People whom leaders assumed were their friends have come to board meetings and accused the board of not caring about the life of the church, of being reckless with the moneys that the congregation had pledged. A simple yet profound project like making sure a sanctuary is handicap accessible turns into a near riot with a few congregation members insisting that the entire membership vote on the plans because they have decided the property committee must have lost its mind. I have had people tell me they were withholding their pledge checks until I stopped doing this or started doing that. I have been accused of heresy more times than I could count. And (here's my favorite) I have been told that the benediction I use "ruins an otherwise perfectly good worship service."

Even if you are not a "crier" like me, both you and I have, at some point, been driven to something like fear and tears. Both of us, at some point, have let them get to us.

And so Paul is encouraging Timothy to get back on the horse and ride. You got bucked off. Fine. Now get back in the saddle. My own personal Paul to Timothy moment came just a few short years ago when an elder at the church I serve sat me down and said, in no uncertain terms, "Stop being afraid. You have a vision from God about where our church can go, and a lot of us are starting to glimpse it, and we want to go there with you. We need to you help us more fully see it. Stop being afraid, and start being the leader God has called you to be."

And so, if I may be so bold, I'd like to be the Paul to your Timothy.

As a congregational leader, the spirit of fear and anxiety that you feel is not from God. God has not called your board to make decisions that align with conventional wisdom or reflect the desires of the same few people. God has called *your specific group* to discern the mind of Christ and the will of God for this time and place together, not to be a rubber stamp for whatever your senior pastor puts in front of you. God has given you all that you need to accomplish the work that God has set out for you to do. Rather than giving you a spirit of fear and anxiety, God has gifted you with boldness and conviction, a willingness to make sacrifices, and the ability to carry through. You have been given power, love, and self-discipline.

Stemming the Tide

But how can we live like people of power, love, and self-discipline? Practically speaking, a few postures and practices can be put into place to make sure information cascades don't take over our leadership boards and to ensure that our boards are able to resist conventional wisdom.

First, the more important the decision, the less likely it is that an information cascade will take hold. When group members are aware that something significant is at stake, they are more serious in their work, and as a result they are less likely to fall into line with what someone else's desires.

It makes sense that if I want to know whether it's going to rain, I could look out my window and see if people are carrying their umbrellas. If I want an idea of what might be a good album to buy this week, I can look at the sales charts and see what everyone else is buying and start there. These kinds of decisions are relatively inconsequential. Sure, I might have to carry around my umbrella all day even if it doesn't rain, or maybe I don't really love that album I just bought. But I can live with that. These are not the most important decisions in my life.

But when it came to naming our four boys? My wife and I were pretty insistent that we stay away from popular names. When it came to deciding where in town we would buy our house? We resisted the flow of buyers in our area to go with new construction. These choices were about things that were important to us. We weren't going to rely on someone else to make the decisions for us.

The same idea applies to churches. Choosing which brand of paper to buy for the copying machine is not really that important a decision, but hiring a choir director is. We're relatively willing to be stuck with a lot of paper for a while, so we might be willing to buy what the office supply sales rep suggests is the best. But hiring an employee requires our full attention and best effort. Even if the person has good references, if we did not feel that the interview matched our expectations, we are less inclined to vote to hire the person.

If you really want to take advantage of the wisdom of a group, make sure that what is before them is important. Don't waste anyone's time by asking a group to make routine decisions. Leave those items to individuals who are closer to the action.

The second practice for making a group smarter is to figure out a way for each person to contribute their private information. Private information is what makes a group smarter, for it provides the group with a fuller range of alternatives from which to choose.

Unless a group is moderated well, not all the cards will be laid on the table. For example, extroverts, who have no problem working through ideas aloud with others, will dominate a discussion, while introverts, who are content to sit and listen, will not contribute unless prompted. What if a vote is called but a critical piece of information, still sitting in an introvert's brain, could redefine the entire issue? Because that introvert never felt they could or would get a word in edgewise, they kept it to themselves, and the group suffers.

One church I was a part of had as one of their group covenants, "We will listen to the prophet in our midst." The belief was that our understanding of the mind of Christ and the will of God may initially come to us from just one person. Therefore, it was incumbent on the group to be vigilant about listening to one another as well as on each of us to be our whole selves and contribute all of our private information.

Often, however, it is not group dynamics that lead people to withhold private information. What is more likely is that the actual structure of the formal decision-making process ensures that most private information is left on the table. Many church groups, in an effort to be effective and efficient, employ some form of parliamentary procedure. I know that I may here raise the ire of many a parliamentarian. I also know that ordered decision-making processes have their place and that their goals are (to steal the subtitle of Robert's Rules of Order) to ensure "courtesy and justice for all." I am not suggesting that we wholly do away with ordered debate, conversation, and decision making.

I am pointing out, however, that by its very nature parliamentary procedure does not allow for true generative discussion, just reactive debate. When a parliamentary body is presented with a "motion," even if the body "amends" it, all they are doing is responding to the movers' idea. Because the momentum of the discussion is behind the original motion, other ideas are rarely heard, let alone considered. Even if a group member manages to get some brief attention for an idea, there is little to no room in structured, ordered debate for a true compromise of ideas. The best a group can hope for is to replace one basic idea with another. If structured debate is all that a group participates in, it is basically a very orderly information cascade.

The question we in the church need to answer, then, is, How do we ensure generative discussion and decision making and, at the same time, ensure that we are ordered so that no one dominates the process? Whatever process we create is going to freak-out the efficiency lovers among us. The mess that is the *Wikipedia* decision-making process takes a lot of time and a lot of sustained attention, but everyone's private information is honored. It is built into the project through the wiki process.

Surowiecki reminds us of the third reality we need to stay aware of to avoid information cascades:

> The fundamental problem with cascades is that choices are made sequentially, instead of all at once. There are good reasons for this— some people are more cautious than others, some are more willing

to experiment, some have more money than others. But roughly speaking, all the problems that cascades can cause are the result of the fact that some people make their decisions before others. If you want to improve an organization's or an economy's decision making, one of the best things you can do is make sure, as much as possible, that decisions are made simultaneously (or close to it) rather than one after another."[8]

I cannot remember the last time I was a part of a group that voted sequentially, but I'm sure that it still happens. If yours is a group that does so, I suggest you heed Surowiecki's advice and stop.

Also, I would suggest that, as much as possible, before the official vote begins, you set aside time for general and somewhat free-flowing conversation during which everyone is given an opportunity to speak to an issue if they wish. The best method I have found for accomplishing this goal is "mutual invitation." The form of mutual invitation I like best is a two-part event.

First, the topic is introduced through communicating pertinent information that everyone present might need to know in order to speak intelligibly on the subject. The topic could be introduced either by one group member or by a committee giving a report. After the initial presentation, another group member is then invited to speak to the topic in whatever way they wish. They may respond to the presentation or suggest an alternate line of thought. When they finish, they then invite another member of the group to do the same until all have had a chance to speak. (It is not required that everyone say something. Anyone can pass.) At this point, I recommend a period of silence, concluding with a prayer before entering into another round of reflection.

Many times a basic outline indicating where a group wants to go emerges, and whoever is moderating the meeting is able to name the patterns to the group. If there is no clear sense of direction, another round of reflection may be entered into or a more free-flowing form of discussion may follow. If there does seem to be consensus on the basic points, structured debate could then be entered into for the purposes of clarifying where the group has indicated it desires to go. (I will discuss this topic more in chapter 6, but an effective moderator is crucial in making sure that an open discussion process has occurred. The moderator must not only guard the independence of each member present but must also have an ear toward patterns that will emerge and be able to offer that feedback to the group at key times and in helpful ways.)

Encouraging independence of thought and ensuring that it is valued is a bedrock value for any group that wishes to act in a wise way. Acknowledging and accepting the specific context each person comes from virtually guarantees that the gifts each person has received from God will be brought to bear. But valuing each person's context has implications well beyond what decisions a group makes. As we will see in the next chapter, valuing different contexts means that leaders give up control in order to unleash and empower the congregation they serve to fully live into their calls to work for the peace, justice, and wholeness God intends for creation.

~ Chapter Five ~

Letting Go, or the Art of Decentralization

I began college in 1994. I had what I would consider the typical college move-in experience. One Saturday morning my entire family loaded into our Chevy conversion van, with all of my worldly possessions crammed in the back, and drove the four hours from Tonganoxie, Kansas, to Sterling, Kansas, for my freshman year at Sterling College. When we arrived, we made our way to my dorm, and when I walked into my room, I felt like I had entered a whole new world.

My roommate had arrived a few days earlier as part of the college's orientation staff, so he had for the most part already moved in and claimed space. Just after we arrived, he came in. His name was J.R. and he was a long-haired sophomore theater major. He had taken the top bunk (which I was fine with) and the closet on the right (bigger and a bit more room) but had left me with the better study desk. He had set up his stereo and word processor and told me that I should feel free to use either at any time. He had also partially decorated. There was a poster for the Velvet Underground (who?), a poster for a film

I had not been allowed to see, and, above the bed, a poster of Robert Smith, lead singer of the Cure. He helped me and my dad carry my stuff in and then excused himself to go help some other folks move in.

After he left, my mom pointed to the poster of Mr. Smith and said, "Landon?!" I was, of course, worried that he was still right out in the hall, but still, the sense of newness was so overwhelming that I didn't really care *that* much. Standing there, in the middle of *my dorm room*, brought a wave of satisfaction and freedom like I had never known. For the first time in my life, I was truly excited to be me in the place where I found myself.

High school had been rough for me, as it usually is for geeks who gravitate toward choir, band, and theater in the Midwest. I was called all the pejorative names that sensitive, artsy-type guys get called. Add to all those characteristics that I was a loudmouth Jesus Freak fundamentalist, and my chances of making a good impression on fellow students were slim. But here, at Sterling College, all those things were cherished and valued. I was there on choir and theater scholarships, and because the school was Christian, I was surrounded by other Jesus Freaks. I could forget the old life; this was the new life, a new start. I felt like I now lived in a new country. Even so, my college career started off with a bit of a fizz. On my first night in college—the first night of the rest of my life—*I went to bed at 11:00 p.m.*

Yes, true—part of it was due to the fact that I was exhausted. At the time I didn't realize I was an introvert and a huge day like that had worn me out. All I knew was that I had a lot of activities to go to the next day, and I wanted to be rested. I am fairly sure that the last thing my mom told me before my family drove away was, "Make sure and get some rest tonight. You've got a big day tomorrow." Great motherly advice (and for the record, Mom, advice I'm glad I took), but—let's be honest—that is not the way an eighteen-year-old man on his first night in college is supposed to behave. It's just . . . *weird*.

In my defense, I was being perfectly consistent with the way I had lived the previous eighteen years of my life. My parents owned a donut shop, and I would often work there with my dad all through the night. I spent my high school years getting up at the crack of dawn to get on a bus and go to debate and forensic tournaments. Sunday morning in my house meant Sunday school, and you were not late. I had learned, fairly quickly, that if something important was happening the next day, you needed to get a good night of sleep beforehand.

So, the next day, when J.R. and the guy who lived next door said to me, "Dude, nobody goes to bed at eleven in college," I was taken aback. Apparently, I had missed the memo. There were rules I didn't know about. There were patterns of behavior and social understandings I needed to catch up on, and I needed to catch up on them quickly.

History Matters

When we change contexts in our lives, it is impossible to simply flip a switch and become and behave like a different person. Where we have been and who we have been taught to be are radically infused in every fiber of our being. We might learn the new behaviors of the place where we now reside, but "they" say old habits die hard, and they are right. Even now, years removed from my "fundagelical" upbringing, preaching the gospel through the lens of open source sometimes makes me wince. The "turn or burn" mentality was so ingrained in me that I still occasionally worry I'm doing something wrong when I proclaim that there is nothing we can or must do to receive the grace and peace of Jesus Christ (or anything else I explained in chapter 1).

Our religious heritage, our high school experiences . . . these things make us who we are, and it is not possible to ever really shut them off. Our history matters, and we have to be aware of it when we embark on the new path God has called us to. Even the people of God had to contend with a major piece of their history: *for many generations, they had lived in Egypt as slaves.*

The Bible never says how many years the people lived as captives to the pharaohs, doing their bidding. All we know is that Joseph's father and brothers had moved there during a famine in order to save their family from starving. And then some time later,

> a new king arose over Egypt, who did not know Joseph. He said to his people, "Look, the Israelite people are more numerous and more powerful than we. Come, let us deal shrewdly with them, or they will increase and, in the event of war, join our enemies and fight against us and escape from the land." Therefore they set taskmasters over them to oppress them with forced labor. They built supply cities, Pithom and Rameses, for Pharaoh. But the more they were oppressed, the more they multiplied and spread, so that the Egyptians came to dread the Israelites. The Egyptians became ruthless in imposing tasks on the Israelites, and made their lives bitter with hard service in mortar and brick and in every kind of field labor. They were ruthless in all the tasks that they imposed on them.
>
> —EXOD. 1:8–14

"Look," Pharaoh said. "There are a lot of Israelites. If we're not careful, they will eventually participate in our demise. Let's get them under our thumb now and control them." The people in power did what people in power almost always do—command and control. This went on for many years, until God sent Moses to free the people and lead them out of oppression.

Not long after the people had crossed the Red Sea comes a pivotal moment in the life of the ancient community. God had cared for the people by providing Moses to lead them to freedom and had ensured that they had water to drink and Manna to eat. Just before they reached Sinai, we are treated to a scene in Exodus 18 in which Moses's father-in-law, Jethro, gives him some practical advice on running the community.

Then Moses told his father-in-law all that the LORD had done to Pharaoh and to the Egyptians for Israel's sake, all the hardship that had beset them on the way, and how the LORD had delivered them. Jethro rejoiced for all the good that the LORD had done to Israel, in delivering them from the Egyptians. Jethro said, "Blessed be the LORD, who has delivered you from the Egyptians and from Pharaoh. Now I know that the LORD is greater than all gods, because he delivered the people from the Egyptians, when they dealt arrogantly with them." And Jethro, Moses' father-in-law, brought a burnt offering and sacrifices to God; and Aaron came with all the elders of Israel to eat bread with Moses' father-in-law in the presence of God.

The next day Moses sat as judge for the people, while the people stood around him from morning until evening. When Moses' father-in-law saw all that he was doing for the people, he said, "What is this that you are doing for the people? Why do you sit alone, while all the people stand around you from morning until evening?" Moses said to his father-in-law, "Because the people come to me to inquire of God. When they have a dispute, they come to me and I decide between one person and another, and I make known to them the statutes and instructions of God." Moses' father-in-law said to him, "What you are doing is not good. You will surely wear yourself out, both you and these people with you. For the task is too heavy for you; you cannot do it alone. Now listen to me. I will give you counsel, and God be with you! You should represent the people before God, and you should bring their cases before God; teach them the statutes and instructions and make known to them the way they are to go and the things they are to do. You should also look for able men among all the people, men who fear God, are trustworthy, and hate dishonest gain; set such men over them as officers over thousands, hundreds, fifties and tens. Let them sit as judges for the people at all times; let them bring every important case to you, but decide every minor case themselves. So it will be easier for you, and they will bear the burden with you. If you do this, and God so commands you, then you will be able to endure, and all these people will go to their home in peace."

—EXOD. 18:8–23

The scene begins with Moses telling Jethro all the ways in which the Lord has cared for the people, especially how they had been delivered. Jethro then offers a prayer of thanksgiving to the Lord for the deliverance of the people. I begin here because I want to point out something about how the text conveys an understanding of God. In the course of three verses, some form of the word *deliver* is used four times to describe God's actions in relation to the people.

This repetition is important. Writing materials in the ancient world were scarce. You couldn't run down to the local office supply store and pick up a new notebook. People wrote not carelessly but with intentionality. They wanted to maximize their resources, so they put as much into the text as they thought necessary but no more than they needed. We might question a student's vocabulary if they wrote *delivered* four times in four sentences, but repetition in the biblical text is a clue for us that something important is being communicated. If it is in the Bible, it is there for a reason.

In this little scene between Moses and Jethro, it is important for us to know that the God they worship and serve is the God who has delivered them. The exodus is still the primary story that informs the identity of the Jewish people, and it is built on the conviction that God is a god who delivers the people. God is about freedom—freedom from oppression, freedom from constant work, freedom from fear. Because of this, it should not strike us as odd that the next day, after Moses "sat as judge for the people, while the people stood around him from morning to evening," Jethro came and questioned the practice. Moses was doing it all, and Jethro knew that the result would not be good.

Now, Moses had good reason for doing what he was doing. As he told his father-in-law, "the people come to me to inquire of God." Essentially, the people did not know what to do, so they came to Moses to ask him what God wanted.

I would like us to pause here and revisit the point we started with. When we move from one context to another, we often find that we are at a loss about how to conduct ourselves in the new context. Something new has occurred, but we only know how to act as if we are still living in the old. Even though the people had been delivered from slavery by God, to some extent they still operated as if they were slaves. Their entire life up to this point had been lived with taskmasters set above them, imposing their will upon them. Every minute of their day—when they rose and when they slept—was accounted for. Their work was laid out for them, and I'm sure that whatever free time they had was uncomfortable for them. They were likely worried that their masters would enter at any moment and force them to do something. They had not been free for very long when this story occurs in the biblical text, and the people are simply trying to live in their new context the only way they know how: by mimicking their old one.

In the old system, someone told them what to do, and so they now turned to their leader Moses to do the same. They recognized that they were ultimately under the authority of the Lord, but they thought the only person who knew what God wanted was Moses. They had replaced one master, Pharaoh, with another, Moses.

I am sure that part of the reason they came to Moses to inquire of God was that they knew this God cared for them, and they wanted to serve their God the best they could. They had no precedent for living in any way other than as slaves, and someone needed to show them. That is what inquiring of God meant. The times in the Bible when people inquired of God were the times when they didn't already know what to do. I think it would be safe to say that the Israelites' slave mentality was kicking in a little bit, and they didn't want to do it wrong.

We cannot fault them for this. Freedom is hard to accept. Only two chapters earlier, God had given the people manna to eat, and part of the instruction was that on the sixth day they needed to gather twice as much manna as usual, because the seventh day was going to be a *sabbath*, a day of rest. In both places where we find the Ten Commandments recorded (Exod. 20 and Deut. 5), the people are told that everyone and everything was going to rest. Sabbath is not only a gift from God but it is also a commandment from God. The reason is that the people are no longer slaves. God wanted them to learn to live as free people, and so they were taught how to do so through an instruction to rest. These early stories are about the people learning what freedom means and how freedom operates in their lives. We now see them learning another lesson about freedom: how to organize themselves.

I see Christians trying not to "do it wrong" all the time. As I have previously discussed, we want to make sure we are doing this thing called church correctly. We see this as a precious gift from God, and we don't want to squander it. We want to be true to what we understand God is asking of us. This is a good impulse. We have seen that this God delivers; we have experienced this God delivering! We realize that we are no longer subject to the whims of oppressors but cared for by a God who loves us. We don't want anyone taking this away. We want to always know that this love and mercy is available.

And so we come to this work of mission and ministry with a sense of responsibility. We want to be as faithful as we can be, so we fall back on the patterns we know and tend to organize ourselves for the sake of the gospel according to the ways we organize ourselves in other areas of our lives. Just as the Israelites were so used to a master telling them what to do that they made Moses their new master, our churches are so used to the centralized, top-down command and control systems of the world that we try to use the same structure in our pursuit of freedom. Jesus spoke of the kingdom of God breaking into our midst and setting people free, but we hear *kingdom* and assume that what God is up to is instituting a new monarchy. We justify it by saying that Jesus is a different kind of king, but we are still taking the authority pattern we already know and trying to make it work differently. To recall the point from the previous chapter, we stick with the tried and true, even though we claim that we are not.

Part of the reason we lie to ourselves like this, I think, is that we fear chaos and crave stability. I have watched over the past several years as author and speaker Phyllis Tickle has taught us about the Great Emergence (a current upheaval in modern Christianity resulting in new forms of theology and practice, comparable to the Great Reformation), and I have witnessed time and again how people react out of fear, because she pushes us to admit that patterns of authority are crumbling. I addressed this in chapter 2 by noting that many people see the openness of *Wikipedia* as anarchy, believing it creates an "anything goes" environment. This could not be further from the truth, but when all people have known is "command and control," we fear anything that doesn't fit our experience.

And so churches centralize authority, but try to make sure those in authority use their power for good. We mimic the same structures of command and control but attempt to use them for a different purpose. This was what the Israelites did as they came out of Egypt, but it wasn't the only time they did it. Later, they begged God for a king so that they could be just like the other nations. "You don't want that," God told them. "A king will not deliver you like I have and continue to do. A king will put you back into servitude. A king will not be good for you."

They Need Me

But, long before that request, Jethro was concerned about too much power being lodged with his son-in-law. He asks, "Why are

you doing this? Why do you sit alone from morning to evening?"
And Moses's answer could be uttered by any congregational
leader anywhere: "Because they need me to." It is not far off
to say that many congregational leaders have big egos. I think
it's fine to speak mainly of pastors here, but the point applies
to anyone: many of us are convinced that we are the linchpin
holding our congregations together.

Let's be clear: it is not a bad thing to say that one has an ego.
Ego is good. Ego is what helps us make it through the day. Ego is
what helps us stand up in front of twenty-five, fifty, one hundred,
one thousand people every Sunday morning and proclaim the
good news of Jesus Christ. Congregational leaders need some
amount of ego to be effective in what God has called us to do.
However, as I have implicitly and explicitly said throughout
this book, we also possess gift, skills, and intelligence *that are
narrow*. Ours is not the only intelligence that is fungible. We
are no different from anyone else.

Bruce Reyes-Chow, former moderator of the General Assembly of the Presbyterian Church (USA), likes to tell a story
about his first call. On his first day at the new church, a longtime
member took him around the building for a tour. They came
to the hallway where the portraits of the various pastors were
hung, and she began telling him a few stories about those who
had served there before him. It was an impressive bunch.

After a while, she pointed to a place next in the line of frames
and said, "And that is where your picture will go." Bruce says
he had a moment of pride, considering the reality that God had
called him to that place to serve those people, of pride that he
had gifts that he was excited to see used with his new congregation. But the woman was not finished. Pointing to a space a
little farther down she said, "And that is where the picture of
the pastor *after you* will go."

Pastors are called to a particular time and place for a season.
We should not forget that point. Some seasons will be longer

than others, but we do God and congregations a disservice if we do not remember that a church was there before we arrived, and a church will be there after we leave.

Moses's answer, however, was fuller than just "they need me." He told Jethro that he sat morning to evening because they needed him to settle disputes, and tell them how God wanted them to live together. The truth was the people needed to be taught, and Moses was the one to teach them. The reason he was the one sitting as judge, all alone, was that no one else knew what to do. Jethro's response provides us with some clarity about why centralizing authority is detrimental to the life of a group.

Jethro calls the spade a spade. "What you are doing is not good." Jethro is an outsider to this community. He is a priest of Midian. He is not wrapped up in the particular politics, nor the established norms and mores of this group. He doesn't know this family and that they have been at each other ever since they left Egypt. He is not distracted by the minutiae that might distract Moses, so he doesn't mince words.

Jethro points out that Moses is going to be worn out. Of course he is. He's doing it all. Sound familiar? Congregational leaders, especially clergy, burn out at an alarming rate. We all know the emotional and psychological effects of burnout, but it seems that the effects that overworked clergy suffer are especially outrageous:

> In May [2010], the Clergy Health Initiative, a seven-year study that Duke University began in 2007, published the first results of a continuing survey of 1,726 Methodist ministers in North Carolina. Compared with neighbors in their census tracts, the ministers reported significantly higher rates of arthritis, diabetes, high blood pressure and asthma. Obesity was 10 percent more prevalent in the clergy group.
>
> The results echoed recent internal surveys by the Evangelical Lutheran Church in America, which found that 69 percent of its

ministers reported being overweight, 64 percent having high blood pressure and 13 percent taking antidepressants.

A 2005 survey of clergy by the Board of Pensions of the Presbyterian Church also took special note of a quadrupling in the number of people leaving the profession during the first five years of ministry, compared with the 1970s.[1]

Why is this happening? I think there are two reasons.

On one side is a systemic problem with what congregations expect clergy to be and do. An earlier chapter has addressed this, but it bears repeating: *pastors are not coming to churches to be the resident church expert.*

There is a huge problem when we expect pastors to fulfill the ministry they have been called to *and be a church administrator.* In recalling the conversations I have had with various pastors, I have never heard one of them say, "I am so excited to be a pastor so that I can be the executive director of a nonprofit corporation!" To be sure, pastors *can* learn the ins and outs of administration, but most pastors understand their roles quite differently from the way the congregation does. Remember the list in chapter 3? Most current congregations expect their pastors to be an expert in all the roles ever attributed to pastoral leadership. Simply put, pastors are not cut out to do the jobs we are asking them to do.

On the other hand is a problem with pastors giving in to the idea that they should be the resident church expert and consequently not effectively training and equipping congregations to fulfill their calling to mission and ministry. Too many pastors overfunction, effectively teaching congregations to underfunction, and then they wonder why members have an unrealistic view of what pastors are called to do.

In response to an August 2010 *New York Times* opinion piece on clergy burnout by United Church of Christ minister Jeffrey MacDonald, blogger and pastor Adam Copeland responds:

It's all about the parishioners, MacDonald says. They're the problem. Somehow he suggests the issue isn't pandering pastors; not
unhealthy-vacation-skipping pastors; not non-exercising hypocritical
pastors; not wealth-consumed pastors; not pastors who fail to study
or teach the Bible; not pastors who fail to lead relevant services or
preach quality sermons; not pastors who forget tradition and take
the easy road out; not pastors who read too little and watch TV too
much; not pastors who would rather be moderating an investment
club than a church council meeting. No, it's somehow all the fault
of the parishioners.

I believe trying to assign blame to either pastors or church
members is foolhardy. I also believe nothing short of a structural
remodel will solve our problem. I want to return to that in a
moment, but first let's look at the second half of Jethro's analysis:
the people will be worn out.

Waiting and Waiting and Waiting . . .

Consider this story:

> A young woman comes to First Church, excited to be a part of
> a new faith community. She feels connected to God through
> the worship, and the education she has taken part in has been
> meaningful. She really desires to respond to God's grace in the
> midst of her new community and sees areas where her passion
> and skills could be utilized. She puts together a plan for a new
> ministry, and because everything must run its course through
> the proper channels, she dutifully submits her proposal to the
> required committee. And then she waits . . . and waits and waits
> and waits. "Sorry" she is told. "All the committee members hap-
> pened to take vacation in the past three to four weeks, and we
> just haven't been able to get everyone together." She tells them

130

she understands and shows up to present her proposal when
they finally do get together.

At that meeting, they spend very little time on the specifics of
her idea, instead wondering if this would work any better than
the similar program they tried a few years back. After delineating
to her why the previous program failed, they vote to recommend
it to the full board of church leaders.

Again, she dutifully waits for the full board to meet, and
when she arrives at their meeting to present her idea, it becomes
apparent that some board members have already determined
that the idea is not one that the church should pursue. A cursory discussion is held—some mention of "lack of funds and
space"—before proceeding to vote no.

Six weeks later, she is attending a new church and leading a
group of people pursuing her ministry idea with funding that she
and that group had pooled together. Ever attentive, the leaders
at First Church offhandedly ask at the next meeting, "Where
has that young girl with that one idea been lately? She left? Well,
I'm glad we didn't approve her plan then—if she has no more
commitment than that."[2]

This story is familiar isn't it? I'm going to assume that some
version of it occurs regularly in many churches, perhaps even
yours. The story may seem extreme, but it is not that far off the
mark in many congregational settings. While recognizing that
most (if not all) congregational leaders are simply trying to be
responsible for the church they have been called to serve, I think
some truths are embedded in this story that we cannot deny,
some tragic flaws are revealed about the way we do business.

Most obviously *it reveals that folks in our congregations have
good ideas and want to live into their calling as disciples.* When the
word of God is preached, people's lives are changed. Words of
freedom embolden and empower us. When our eyes are finally

opened to the ways in which the world works—ways that promote selfishness and oppressions—we find that we have an amazing drive to help set things to right. Justice becomes a passion.

In the congregation I serve, it was the proclamation of the word of God that inspired a couple to begin the seventh Habitat for Humanity chapter in the world and inspired another couple to begin a finance and lifestyle education program that we are still deeply involved in. Just a few weeks ago, the cumulative effects of the word of God inspired a member of ours to begin pursuing early retirement so that he could "start doing what God put me on this earth to do." And these are just some examples I know about. Churches are full of passionate women and men who love God and want to live their lives as committed disciples of Jesus. There is no short supply of these folks.

The story reveals that, more often than not, our structures hinder these passionate women and men from pursuing the mission of God. Let's lay aside the wisdom of organizational checks and balances (which is a vital task) for one moment. In trying to shepherd an idea for ministry and mission through the various processes our churches employ, many people experience a great amount of frustration. They find they have to jump through a lot of hoops and attend a lot of meetings. They could probably stomach these steps if it weren't for the fact these steps are the very things that communicate to them that their church believes someone else has better opinions about their idea than they do.

As I have discussed before, our systems are largely built with the assumption that the best and smartest among us are or will be in positions of authority and power. We make sure the ideas members generate come before this group of experts, who pass judgment on their viability. I have sat in these sorts of meetings. Very little discussion about the underlying theology of the idea happens. Very little discussion about how it might fit into the larger mission direction of the congregation happens. Usually the discussions center on money, time, space, and volunteers: Do we have enough of each to pull it off?

All of this belies a belief in the fungibility of intelligence. Rather than trust the one closest to the ground to work out the details, a group of people who more than likely started thinking about the idea right before the meeting when they were looking through their agendas get to pass judgment on the passion of the person sitting across from them at the table.

The story reveals that a lot of churches see congregational leaders as the gatekeepers of the church's mission rather than unleashers of it. Members of congregations have a lot of ideas about how to be the people of God, and many times it seems that congregational leaders see their job as making sure no one "goes off the deep end." A culture of micromanagement will stifle any mission or ministry that a member might try to start.

I will discuss this more later, but studies have shown that people yearn to experience autonomy as they pursue meaning and purpose. People want to contribute to the goodness of the world, and they want to be free to pursue that contribution without you or me communicating to them that we know better than they do. The vast majority of the times in my life when I have been most dissatisfied with my work occurred when I was being micromanaged. And, yes, many of those instances occurred as a part of my ministry. But I am a paid staff member of a church. Because I have been hired to accomplish certain goals, I have recognized that some amount of micromanagement is going to occur and I have accepted it. But those who wish to pursue mission and ministry in our congregations do not have to accept it. And yet, we treat those who want give of their time and talents as if they are brand-new employees who need breaking in. Is it any wonder that it is hard to find volunteers?

Finally, the story reveals that congregational leaders are living with a scarcity mindset. There is only so much to go around. I want us to remember that our leaders are good people who have been asked to do what they see as an important job, and one of those jobs is allocating resources. The simple fact is that a congregation cannot do everything everyone wants it to do. And yet, when the only concern of a church board is the bottom line and how many pledges are being paid, we reveal that we are very afraid of not having enough resources. We make the assumption that a lack of financial resources means we cannot pursue the mission of God.

What is truly tragic, however, is that a dip in finances makes us behave in an insular manner. We begin obsessing about the maintenance of our buildings and the purity of our doctrines (because, surely, that must be the reason people are not giving). We start focusing on the *lack* of resources and fail to recognize the powerful growth potential present if we would try to pursue mission and ministry that were not dependent on finances.

So, is Jethro right? Will our current organizational structure wear the people out?

Have you ever waited at the department of motor vehicles (DMV)? I live in a smallish town, and even I dread going to the DMV. About a year ago I had to go there to get the tags on my cars renewed. I showed up, dutifully took a number, and sat down to wait my turn. The chairs were uncomfortable. Babies were crying. The space was very hot that day (or was it overly cold? I can't remember . . .), and I was miserable. After forty minutes or so, I was called up to the counter and had a conversation with a very nice but very tired woman who saw me as no more than number 198. I told her what I needed, and she proceeded to tap-tap-tap on her keyboard, asking me questions I readily provided answers for. She asked for my paperwork, which I presented, and she shuffled through. Then . . . she sighed.

"Sir, I'm sorry, but I can't process your request right now."

"What?"

"I'm sorry, sir, but I cannot process your request right now. You don't have what you need." She pointed to one of the zillion posters on the wall. "As you can see right there, to obtain license tags for your vehicles, you need to have The Absolute Right Document That You Don't Have. I can't do anything for you unless you have that document. You need to go get it and come back." I stared at her.

"Next! One-ninety-nine!"

Now, there was nothing that could be done. I didn't have what I needed to get what I needed. This much is true. But even if I had, the entire process was *exhausting*. Waiting around, doing nothing is, oddly, very taxing. You feel like you're in a perpetual state of "Get ready . . ." You're on alert, and it takes a toll on your well-being. Waiting is hard.

For several years, our family's income has been low enough that our children have qualified for government assistance, specifically the Women, Infant, and Children (WIC) food program. Because my wife and I are caring parents and like it when our four boys' bellies are full, we went through the process of registering for the program. It is exhausting. Regular checkups with a nutritionist. Regular verification of income. Lots of waiting. But, in this instance, the really taxing part is the humiliation. Showing up to the health department office to pick up food vouchers that we have to then take to the grocery store and present is just about the most humiliating thing I have ever experienced in my entire life. I am not being hyperbolic. I know many people who don't sign up for that very reason. Yes, I am grateful, and yes, I have pumped myself up for years to do it. But my wife and I struggle with the message implicit in our participation in the program—that *we can't do it*. Every month we fight the feeling that we are not good providers for our children, even though we are highly educated people who make many sacrifices and live according to a tight budget. I'm not seeking pity here. Rather, I want to illustrate what happens when the structures society puts into place communicate to people that *they can't do it*.

There is nothing you and I can do about the DMV or WIC. Those agencies are the way they are. But the church is different.

We cannot continue to structure ourselves in such a way that, when the people of God are inspired by the proclamation of God's word and their hearts are set aflame to pursue peace, justice, and wholeness in the world, we tell them they need to settle down and wait for a while. We must stop structuring ourselves in such a way that faithful and passionate women and men are told someone else must first pass judgment on the viability of their idea. We cannot continue practices that scream a belief in a world of scarce resources when our churches are full of people ready and aching to be Christ's disciples.

Yes, we have worn our people out. And here's a secret: *Although we have worn many people down into automatons, waiting for our instructions, many more are going to pursue the mission of God with or without us.* Wouldn't you rather they do it with us?

Authority at the Point of Gift

I don't want to suggest the central theme of this book—that a group of people can make better decisions than the best person in the group—be set aside. I am not all of a sudden advocating a move from the group to the individual, nor am I suggesting systems of accountability somehow be ignored. I am suggesting, based on the flaws inherent in a centralized system and on our values and convictions as the people of God, that we should begin to focus our energies on creating new structures and transforming old ones to take advantage of the power of *decentralization*. James Surowiecki defines this sometimes slippery term for us:

> What do we mean by "decentralization," anyway? It's a capacious term, and in the past few years it's been tossed around more freely than ever. Flocks of birds, free-market economies, cities, peer-to-peer computer networks: these are all considered examples of decentralization. Yet so, too, in other contexts, are the American public-school

system and the modern corporation. These systems are dramatically different from each other, but they have this in common: in each, power does not fully reside in one central location, and many important decisions are made by individuals based on their own local and specific knowledge rather than by an omniscient or farseeing planner.[3]

I have endeavored to promote decentralization in my congregation. For each of the four years I have served my congregation, we have had a different elder serve as the chair of our stewardship and finance committee. I always introduce the role to the new chairperson this way: "I went to seminary, not business school. Now, I have ideas and opinions about a lot of things, and many of those things are, of course, informed by the training I've had in theology, biblical studies, and organizational dynamics. But I did not get into ministry to create financial spreadsheets or analyze insurance plans. I'll make you a deal: you take care of the books, and I'll take care of The Book."

A smile usually creeps across the new chair's face when I say this, because it communicates something to him or her that is vitally important in a church setting: *I trust you.* These are people who have been called by God through the voice of a congregation to be servants of that congregation for a time. They have the qualities that God desires for leaders. Why would anyone not trust them?

A few years ago our congregation constituted a board of deacons. We had not had deacons in thirty-plus years. In our denomination, deacons are those charged with leading the ministry of care and compassion, but they are subject to the review and oversight of our session (board of elders). Yet, even though this hierarchical relationship exists, members of the session have understood that the gifts God has given the deacons are not the gifts that they themselves possess. Because of that, the deacons have been given wide latitude to pursue their calling in whatever way they see fit. Now, when you ask a member of our church what God is doing in our midst, the first thing you often hear is about the deacons. They are doing far more than the session could have ever imagined, because the session was wise enough to give them wide berth and trust the tacit knowledge present in those called to diaconal service.

Tacit knowledge is "knowledge that can't be easily summarized or conveyed to others, because it is specific to a particular place or job or experience, but is nonetheless tremendously valuable."[4] This is what a decentralized system is built upon. Covenant Community Church in Louisville, Kentucky, where I did most of my field education in seminary, has a saying: *Authority at the Point of Gift*. If the community discerned that someone was particularly gifted in a certain area, we released her to do that work and to lead us in it. This group is gifted in music, so we release them to provide the music for our community. This person is good with administrative details, so we give him the responsibility to shepherd that process for us. Trusting someone's tacit knowledge brings benefits to the entire community.

It is interesting to sit and talk to our deacons. Ask them to explain what they do, and they offer answers that they themselves say sound a little "fluffy." One deacon spoke of being with someone at a crucial time, but how did she know to be there? She doesn't know, she just *knew*. Another talks of saying the right thing at the right time. How did you know to say that? I just *knew*. The deacons get flustered when pressed for specifics, because in the ministry of being present to others, you can't often delineate what's going on. Sure, they can talk about the procedure for making hospital visits, but their ministry is more about being in tune and connected with people than anything else.

What is most interesting is that trusting another person or group to do this work means they become highly skilled at it. It breeds a sort of specialization, a specific area in which they feel they are contributing meaning and purpose where there was none before. As Surowiecki points out, political philosopher

Adam Smith helped us see that specialization makes people more productive and efficient. When we are allowed the autonomy to do something, we generally arrive at the best way to get it done. Empowering people to do good work means that they *will* do good work.

Knowing the Difference between Big Things and Little Things

What was Jethro's advice to his son-in-law? Teach the people the things of the Lord. Then find some good, honest people, and put them in charge of smaller groups. Let those leaders deal with the little things, and when there are big things to sort out, they can bring those to you. If you put this system in place, you all will be able to do anything God calls you to.

The key to good, faithful organization is to create structures where the smallest possible group of people is empowered to do what God is calling for with as little obstruction as possible. We have to break up our top-heavy structures and replace them with loose, open, and nimble ones. Fluid structures can react much more quickly to the changes in need and opportunity. We have to learn the difference between the big things and the little things and give different people the responsibility to deal with each of them. Jethro told Moses that if he did this the people would live in peace, and the Bible indicates that is exactly what happened.

However, one issue remains: How do we ensure that all of these little groups of people don't fly off in any old direction? How do we make sure these efforts are at least somewhat in line with one another and in line with what we understand God to be calling the church to be and do? How do we coordinate the passion without resorting to centralized command and control?

~ Chapter Six ~

Leaders Lead, but Experts Do What, Exactly?

I think it is a fairly safe assumption to make to say that most of us had parents who wanted to make sure our lives were better than they ones they lived. I know I can say that. Sure, my parents screwed up. I was their first kid, so of course they screwed up. But my parents gave me a lot and tried the best they could to teach me how to live a good, responsible, and happy life.

I was fortunate growing up to have many people in my life who helped my parents with that task. My grandparents lived very close by, and I saw my aunts and uncles regularly. We also had close family friends whom my siblings and I referred to as Grandma and Grandpa as well as some we called Aunt and Uncle. I knew firsthand that it takes a village to raise a child.

But I want to say that the most influential and effective helper my parents had was not a flesh-and-blood person in our lives. No, the most effective helper my parents had in raising me was a television character. I would have to say that if I had a second set of parents, they would have to be Heathcliff and Clair Huxtable. That's right. My second dad was Bill Cosby.

Bill Cosby infused my childhood. When I was too young to drive but had theater rehearsals out of town, my mom would drive me there. On those trips we would inevitably cry because we were laughing so hard at the Bill Cosby stand-up comedy routines on the cassettes we listened to in the car. *The Cosby Show* was an event in our house. My family would gather around the television, dance to the opening theme song, and laugh so hard our sides split.

Several episodes of show are burned into my brain, but none stands out like the episode in which Theo, Heathcliff and Clair's son, kept complaining that he could do things on his own and didn't need his parents' advice or help. What parents do not have to deal with a teenager who claims that he or she can live life just fine on his or her own? This episode was brilliant.

After complaining to his parents about the boundaries they were putting on him, Theo woke up the next day to find that his house had been transformed into an alternate reality of sorts in which his family members were portraying different characters in someone's life—a landlord, a boss, and so forth. I remember watching as Theo got paid for whatever job he did and then had to turn around and pay for his rent, food, and other things, leaving him with practically nothing. In several scenes Theo was given a chance to see if he actually could survive on his own, but, in the end, he apologized to his parents because he recognized he wasn't yet ready for the responsibility he had thought he wanted.

Because of that episode (which I'm sure I saw several times through reruns), I never once dared to suggest to my parents that I could care for myself in the same way they did. I never once assumed I was capable of supporting myself, and, although I flirted with crossing several other lines, I never once crossed that one. Theo's experience became a life lesson for me.

I don't want to suggest that I was a perfect kid or am a perfect adult. Far from it. However, even when I fail in some endeavor, I am keenly aware that the reason I did was because I had a faulty assumption going in. Nine times out of ten, the primary reason I screwed up was not because I was somehow being malicious but because my understanding of a given situation did not reflect the reality of the situation.

Even now, in my life and ministry, the reason I fall short of my goals or expectations is because I have a wrong read on the context. I also believe that the primary reason why mainline churches are struggling to have an impact on their communities is a direct result of not having a right read on their context. In being unaware of (or ignoring) the trend toward decentralization, churches continue to insist that a small group of people must vet or generate every idea to be associated with a congregation. But decentralization requires more than just a change in structure. It also requires that congregational leaders function in some fundamentally different ways.

Telling Jesus What to Do

In the tenth chapter of Mark, the disciples made the same mistake I watched Theo Huxtable make. Two of them, James and John, had a specific idea of what it meant to be a leader, and they tried to get Jesus to give in to their way of seeing the world.

> James and John, the sons of Zebedee, came forward to him and said to him, "Teacher, we want you to do for us whatever we ask of you." And he said to them, "What is it you want me to do for you?" And they said to him, "Grant us to sit, one at your right hand and one at your left, in your glory." But Jesus said to them, "You do not know what you are asking. Are you able to drink the cup that I drink, or be baptized with the baptism that I am baptized with?" They replied, "We are able." Then Jesus said to them, "The cup that I drink you will drink; and with the baptism with which I am baptized, you will

be baptized; but to sit at my right hand or at my left is not mine to
grant, but it is for those for whom it has been prepared."

—MARK 10:35–40

James and John, two fishermen brothers and disciples of Jesus,
are following Jesus down the road on the way to Jerusalem.
Sometime before, their colleague Peter had nailed the trivia
question "Who do you say that I am?" with the right answer:
"You are the Messiah." Shortly after that, these brothers were
part of the little band of three who got to be on the mountain
when Jesus was transfigured. They got to see their master with
Elijah and Moses. If they ever had any doubt that this man was
the real deal sent from God, they had no doubt now.

I'm sure that this idea about Jesus had been marinating in
their brains ever since. "Can you believe it? The Son of God
is our rabbi! How cool is that? How cool are we?" They were
walking with God come to earth. That must mean something
was really special about them, too, right? God wouldn't hang
out with just any one.

And so one day they asked Jesus to make it official: "Jesus,
we want you to give us something: Let one of us sit on your
right and the other on your left when we enter glory." They assumed it was appropriate to make the request. Jesus had already
shut Peter down when they had been on the mountain (surely
Jesus wouldn't want *that kind of guy* in an important position).
Besides, there were two of them and Jesus had two places to sit
next to him. It just made perfect sense.

Ever the good teacher, Jesus asks them a question to set the
hook before going on. "You have no idea what you're asking.
Do you think you're going to be able to do what I have to do,
resulting in a place of glory?"

I'm sure they didn't even skip a beat. "Yep. You bet."

Theologian Bill Loader makes a very astute observation about
this passage: "This story is almost bizarre, until we realise that

it parodies that almost universal malady: the will to power. The irony bleeds before us as we hear the ambition of James and John and catch a glimpse of the crucifixion scene. Yes, they can drink the cup. Yes, they can share the baptism. They are the first of many witnesses to misunderstand Jesus and the sacraments. They have got it so wrong."[1] In their drive to be at Jesus's side, the brothers fall victim to a classic case of blind ambition. They are eager for power, although they can't see what they are getting into. As Jesus said, "You don't know what you are asking."

Jesus has already made several earlier points about greatness and what it truly is. He had already taught the disciples about it when he found them arguing over who among them was the greatest. He drops the ever lovely "first must be last" line on them (Mark 9:35). In that scene, he connects greatness with being willing to welcome and care for children, who were considered worthless in the biblical era. Were James and John absent from class that day?

Later he makes *another* point using children, this time telling those gathered that "for it is to such as these that the kingdom of God belongs" (Mark 10:14). Immediately following in the text, Jesus and the disciples encounter a rich man whom Jesus declares not ready for the kingdom because the man demonstrated his unwillingness to part with his possessions. Possessions were considered a sign of blessing from God, so the disciples were confused about who *is* able to enter the kingdom, if not the rich man. Jesus ends his conversation with the disciples by repeating his "first shall be last" teaching. Did James and John miss all these lessons too? How is it that they could be so blind?

I'm convinced it is because they have a faulty understanding of Jesus's authority, and, therefore, a faulty understanding of what it means to have authority. They see Jesus as a man with power, and they want to be near him to take part in and benefit from that power. As Bill Loader points out, at least the intentions of these two brothers makes sense based on where they came from. What more could you expect from two fishermen who have probably never been well off? They live their life only barely more respected than shepherds (and that's not saying much), and one day a rabbi (someone who is respected, a leader in the community) says, "Come, follow me." The entire point of following a rabbi is *to be like the rabbi, to become a leader.* The problem here is not that they're selfish; it's that they have a wrong read on what power is and how it functions.

Who Is God?

When I teach theology in my congregation, I try to make sure that those in the class understand the ways in which our thinking about certain things affects our thinking about other things. If each of us believes we understand ourselves based on who God is, then it is imperative that we have a correct understanding of God. I am notorious for asking, "If that is what you say you want to believe, what does that say about who you understand God to be?" Our God image has a direct impact on the particular way we live our lives.

James and John have their God image wrong. For their entire lives, they have understood God through a lens of awesome and absolute power. Their God was the god of the whole world. All things were subject to their god. You did not mess with their god. How else could their god have brought them out of Egypt? How else could God have sent them *to* and brought them home *from* exile in Babylon? Do you see? We can't completely fault them for the way they understood God, but Jesus was not content to let them continue with that understanding. They weren't home sick during the previous lessons. They were just having trouble adjusting their thinking, and Jesus used their misguided request as an opportunity to help them see God differently.

Christians today have this same issue. Despite the biblical text being replete with varied images of God, most of our practical, functional language about God identifies God in much the same way James and John understood God. Brian Wren, a professor of worship and a hymn writer, makes the point that if we were to look solely at our hymnals, we would be faced with a striking reality: Apparently, the only way we think we can understand God is as "King LAFAP, King-Lord-Almighty-Father-and-Protector."[2] If this is who God is, James and John probably reasoned, shouldn't that be what we strive to be?

We also seek out positions of power and advantage. We tell ourselves that if we are called by God to be a *leader* in various settings, then we must fulfill our duties as a leader in the same way we understand God operating. We, too, must be a "King-Lord-Almighty-Father-and-Protector." While we want to use our power for good, we still operate with the understanding that we have the power and we will do with it what we wish. When this God image is dominant, the entire task of congregational leadership is put in jeopardy because mission and ministry are eclipsed by power struggles.

You're Not the Boss of Me

Even though I was fortunate enough to learn a valuable lesson from watching Theo Huxtable on *The Cosby Show*, I would be lying if I said I did not understand the impulse driving that character. At some point, all of us look at our parents and not so subtly inform them, "You're not the boss of me."

Fortunately, in our teens we have an excuse for this behavior. Developmentally, we are entering a time in which we are stretching our wings. We are starting to experience the drive toward autonomy, which I discussed in the previous chapter. We are starting to live into the understanding that will take us through the rest of our lives: *I have the ability to make decisions.*

This understanding is the bedrock of self-identity for many of us. We know ourselves to be capable people. We have succeeded in the past, and we will continue to succeed. We have a track record, and that track record enables us to make a very significant, yet detrimental, leap: not only do we believe we know what is best for our own lives but also we just might know what is best for others. As such, we seek out positions of power in order to enact our schemes. That we're not the only ones behaving like this is not surprising, so life becomes a fight for dominance.

This is exactly what resulted from the request of James and John. Mark 10:41 is a short verse that Mark seems to use as a transition to Jesus's main point, but it reveals something significant about how we react when faced with a potential loss of status and autonomy: "When the ten heard this, they began to be angry with James and John."

We don't know the specifics of what made them angry, but there it is, plain as day: *they were angry*. Could it be because they had always suspected James and John were two of Jesus's favorites, and they were worried that Jesus was going to make a decision based on that? Were they angry that they didn't think of asking first? Were they angry because they didn't realize the contest had begun? Were they angry because they thought that the contest was supposed to be conducted in a gentlemanly manner? Were they angry because they were all despised by society and couldn't bear the thought of one of them achieving higher status? What was Peter's reason? Hadn't he been the one who correctly named Jesus as the Messiah? Wasn't he the one who was always striking out before anyone else in order to be the faithful disciple? Shouldn't he have been given the recognition James and John sought? The possible reasons are endless, but the result is still the same: they were angry.

I know if I were in that group, I would be angry because of the fact that I knew James and John. I would know all their faults and flaws. I would know what they were good at and what they were not. As soon as I heard their request, I would have been comparing myself to them, if I had not already done so. As soon as I heard the request, I would have set myself against them.

This is what seeking out power does to us—it sets up a dynamic of opposition and conflict. Every time a group is formed, a shuffling occurs to see who is going to come out on top. Who's going to be in charge? Most of the time, we're polite about the struggle, but it is a very real struggle nonetheless. We assert ourselves in ways that demonstrate our power. We may overreach in order to call another's bluff as they strive for the same slot. Eventually the dust settles and a winner emerges, but not before much discomfort and anger take root.

Seeking power or acting as if you rightfully deserve power is divisive. Yes, you may argue that power is necessary to accomplish goals effectively and efficiently, and you may be right. But the fact remains that seeking power and authority assumes a zero-sum game. "I am in charge, and you are not. You will do what I say, or you will suffer the consequences." *This divisive behavior is the opposite of how we are called to act as ministers of reconciliation.*

Paul tells us in Colossians that, in Christ, "the fullness of God was pleased to dwell," and that in and through Christ, "God was pleased to reconcile . . . all things" to God's self (Col. 1:19–20). In 2 Corinthians Paul does not stop with *Christ's* reconciling action but makes it plain that we have been given the "ministry of reconciliation" (2 Cor. 5:18). We are called to carry out Christ's work. How? By imitating Christ, who, as Paul tells us in Philippians,

> *though he was in the form of God,*
> *did not regard equality with God*
> *as something to be exploited,*
> *but emptied himself,*
> *taking the form of a slave,*
> *being born in human likeness.*

And being found in human form,
he humbled himself
and became obedient to the point of death—
even death on a cross.

—PHIL. 2:6–8

Christ pursued reconciliation even to the point of death, and
he pursued it through and with humility. This is the message
he was trying to teach his disciples when they argued over who
was the greatest, and by lifting up children, and by judging the
rich man not yet ready for the kingdom of God. As we will see,
it is this posture of servanthood that Jesus was after, and it is the
posture his church continues to teach. However, it is antithetical
to how the rest of the world operates.

We Do It Differently

Let's go back to the discussion from chapter 3 about the relationship between the church and business. In so many areas of
church organizational life, I believe that part of the problem we
in the church have is that we unreflectively mimic what we see
played out in the business world. "Business" is hard to avoid,
because it affects so much of our lives.

Now whether or not we like the effect business has had on
the church, we must still deal with business's influence. To rip a
Bible verse completely out of context: we live *in* the world but
we are not *of* the world. We must attend to certain realities that
require us to draw upon the knowledge and experience of the
business community. We must take into account certain regula-
tory processes and procedures. We would be foolish not to learn
about good accounting practices and hiring procedures. Even
though the church is an organization built on trust, refusing to
do a background check on a youth group volunteer is criminal
in all senses of the word.

This tension between being a church and taking advantage of business wisdom was brought home to me during my last year of seminary. Graduating seniors were gathered for one of our regular seminars that prepared us to move into ministry settings, and the speaker was a recent graduate who had been an attorney during his first career. His speech was about protecting ourselves from accusations regarding sexual harassment or worse. I will never forget it. He began by saying, "I hate that, as a church, we have to have this talk. But we live in a litigious society, and even though you are all good people, we must do what we can to make sure people are protected. Even if it is from you."

The lessons the church has learned from business in those areas have been invaluable. Businesses are in the business of making money, and so, when dealing with inefficiencies of any kind, businesses usually find a solution pretty quickly. Their experience is helpful to the church, and it is experience we must draw from. However, as I have said, there is a difference between using the practices of business and operating as a business.

The difference is a matter of intentionality. When we know what practices we are using and to what end, there is no problem. Having a good and fair hiring process because we want to make sure that we make ourselves available to *whatever* God might be up to is fantastic. Doing routine background checks on new employees and volunteers is wise because we understand that our first responsibility is always to people who cannot defend themselves. Requiring that employees of the church report any harm that befalls children or vulnerable adults who cannot defend themselves is the right thing to do, not only for the victims' sake but also to teach us a lesson about care and compassion. But when we employ modern business practices unreflectively, we begin to internalize the value systems from which those practices spring. For instance, when we unreflectively obsess over income and expenses, before long we begin to make significant ministry decisions based primarily on the financial bottom line. The self-

protective characteristics of modern business practices can lead a
church to lock up their playground rather than make it available
to the neighborhood children during the week. The fear of being
sued if someone were to get hurt on the swings outweighs the
conviction that their resources are to be used for the betterment
of a neighborhood that does not have a public park nearby.

I believe this is part of what Jesus was trying to teach us when
he told parables contrasting the ways of God and the ways of the
world. He was teaching us a new value system, a new posture,
a new set of behaviors. In his day and age he used the phrase
kingdom of God to concretize this new way of being. He was saying, in effect, "The kingdoms of this world may behave this way,
but the 'kingdom' of God advocates another way." However, I
believe that kingdoms and other political institutions no longer
hold the same level of power and influence over us as they once
did. Whereas the church used to see the state as its main rival
for humanity's allegiance, today it is the economy. Every day we
demonstrate our devotion to and dependence on one corporation
or another. Twenty-four-hour financial channels are some of the
most watched outlets on television. People live and die by the
fluctuations in the stock market. We cannot get away from the
business of doing business. Rather than speaking of the kingdom
of God, I think we should begin teaching people about the Multinational Corporation of God. But what does the Multinational
Corporation of God do that is different? For my purposes here, it
utilizes a different set of values and practices regarding leadership.
When Jesus saw that the request of James and John made the
other disciples angry, he called them together and began laying
out some differences. He told them, "You know that among the
Gentiles those whom they recognize as their rulers lord it over
them, and their great ones are tyrants over them" (Mark 10:42).

No bones about it, Jesus is saying. The Gentile leaders are
about command and control. Those in power constantly demonstrate their power and require their will to be done. Some of

their leaders might solicit input from those they lead, but there is never any question about who is in authority. Jesus also points out that, in the Gentile world, if you want to achieve the highest of heights, you have to be very good at command and control. "Tyrants" he calls them.

As Jesus draws a distinction between tyrannical rulers and his idea of a ruler, we should pay careful attention to one detail. Jesus names the leaders who operate in this way "Gentiles." To a Jew of Jesus's time, the term *Gentile* did not specify a particular group of people. Jesus was not speaking of a certain ethnic or religious group. Nor was he referring to a specific nationality. To a Jew, a Gentile was simply someone who was not in relationship with God. Yes, there were those then (as there are now) who would take a further step and use someone's status as either Jew or Gentile to determine their worth. However, at its simplest, being a Gentile merely meant you were not a Jew.

Jesus makes this distinction because he is trying to make clear to his friends that, because they claim to be the people of God, they have agreed to participate in a particular way of life. They take part in the covenant. At this point, Gentiles choose not to. They are not Jews and they are not claiming to be. So, Jesus says, because we are the people of God, we must always remember that we have been called to be different—to live according to a way that is *better*: more peaceful, more inclusive, more whole, more complex (we should never settle for simplistic reductions), more just. We live this way because we understand ourselves to be the people that God has called and created to live this way. In my denomination, we communicate this truth this way: "The Church of Jesus Christ is the provisional demonstration of what God intends for the world."[3]

We are God's demonstration classroom. We are to be the place where the world can see how it is *supposed* to work. If people want to see what the world *should* be like, they *should* be able to look at the church for the answer. However, because we have forgotten or ignored this distinction, we instead behave just like the Gentiles. I think this tendency to behave like Gentiles can manifest itself in three different ways in the congregational leadership's understanding of their roles.

First, *congregational leaders believe that their job is to be the gatekeepers or the clearinghouse.* As I noted in the previous chapter, many leaders see themselves as the only defense against a rogue congregation member embarrassing the church (at best) or ruining its reputation (at worst). If they can prevent that, then they feel they have done their job.

In their better moments, however, the leaders see themselves more as a clearinghouse. They operate without the fear, but the need for control is still present. They think that before anything is done it has to be cleared with them. Ostensibly this is to ensure that all missions and ministries are aligned, but I have never been in a congregational setting where this idea was present and the underlying motive was not the unwillingness to let go.

Second, *congregational leaders believe their job is to be idea factories and to recruit others to enact their plans.* This is generally the model that church boards adopt, particularly in smaller congregational settings. What can we do? is the question of the day. "Does anyone have any idea as to what the fellowship committee can do? Oh, yeah—we haven't had a progressive dinner in a while. We could do that. Does anyone know who might be good to head that up?"

This model draws heavily on the belief in the fungibility of intelligence. Because *we* are the ones that have been elected to lead, therefore *we* should be the ones to come up with the game plan (the underlying assumption being that part of the reason someone is elected as a leader is because they are good at planning programs). The result is a congregation that does not take any kind of initiative for advancing the kingdom of God because they have been conditioned to believe that their job is to come to worship or attend events, "pay their membership dues," and wait to be entertained, with the caveat that they will occasionally be asked to help.

Third, and a variation of the second understanding, *congregational leaders believe their job is to be idea factories and to enact the plans themselves.* To my mind, this variation is more dangerous than the original. At least the previous understanding got others involved. In this scenario, a small group of tireless people come up with ideas and then put on a show of ministry and mission for their congregation. For the duration of their term, they spend countless nights at the church *doing* programming for the members and eventually wear themselves out. When church leaders act like this, the congregation rarely sees them once their commitment has ended.

But the worst part is that this understanding reinforces the idea that congregation members are obligated to do ministry only at certain times. The rest of the time, we reason, we should be able to sit back and *be the recipients* of the ministry being done. We don't need to serve in the nursery (or teach Sunday school or vacation Bible school or . . .), because we already did it when our kids were little. We don't need to help with the potluck, because we did it when we were on the committee. We don't need to help serve at the soup kitchen, because we did it when we were a part of missions. Been there, done that.

This understanding of leadership is all about creating and controlling content. In the eyes of congregations who understand leadership this way, a leader's job is to ensure that there is something to do. This is also part of what feeds the notion that our leaders are experts, that they are supposed to know how to create things for the church to do. So when members enter into leadership with this understanding, they reason that to not provide these kinds of experiences would be to shirk their responsibilities. Why else, the congregation asks, would we be giving our money if not to have the leadership provide us with some experiences, to create content?

Yet, according to Jesus's understanding, one should not have to wait until he or she is an elected leader before heading up mission projects or ministry programs. Contrary to what most churches do, Jesus tells us that becoming an official leader in a church means giving up our right to head up anything.

Servant Leadership

"But," Jesus says to his disciples, "it is not so among you; . . . whoever wishes to become great among you must be your servant, and whoever wishes to be first among you must be slave of all" (Mark 10:43–44).

Jesus is not giving the disciples the inside track on true corporate advancement. I have heard countless preachers over the years who would like us to believe Jesus is dispensing advice on getting ahead, but that's just not the case. The point Jesus is making is that, in contrast to the Gentile leaders, when we are in positions of leadership we should understand and enact our role properly. The role of servants is to provide their masters with various kinds of support so that the masters can achieve the goals they have. To be someone's slave is to understand that your role is to do what the master needs done without expecting any reward or recognition. Given this understanding, *leading in a congregation does not mean dictating and directing others in mission and ministry but enabling and empowering others to engage in mission and ministry themselves.*

Jesus could not have been clearer on this point than when he said to them, "For the Son of Man came not to be served but to serve, and to give his life as a ransom for many" (Mark 10:45). Here is where the final death blow to James and John's God image comes. By naming himself "the Son of Man" (which was almost synonymous in the Jewish imagination with Messiah), he is saying, "If you want to see how it is that God has determined to 'save' you, then pay attention, for it will be nothing like what you have been expecting. I am going to *save* you by *serving* you."

This short verse tells us a lot about how Jesus understood his ministry. He came not to be served but to serve. He did not show up expecting to be waited on; rather, he intends to be the one doing the waiting. He did not expect to walk down the street and have people fawn all over him for his greatness. No, his way is to go to those whom no one fawns over and make them whole again. "I did not come to boss you around. I came to enable and empower you to be the person God has called and created you to be."

But he doesn't stop there. Jesus makes clear that he will not only enable and empower us but he will also give his life as "a ransom for many." With this simple phrase he is demonstrating for the disciples what servant leadership looks like in totality. Just as he is willing to give up his very life, he is also willing to die to certain needs and wants and desires in order to see others living out the desires of their hearts, desires that God has placed within them. And when he says, "For the Son of Man came," he is saying, "This is who I am (as your rabbi), and so this is who I expect you to be." Because Jesus acts this way, we are to act this way.

Now, I know that we believe this understanding to be true. I know that when we hear sermons about Jesus's call for us to give ourselves up for others, we believe them and want to live out that call. I believe that most of us try to live this way. But this call is not only for us as individuals, it is also for us as a group—a gathered community of faith. It is not only illogical and inconsistent but also *sinful* for us to simply allow our personal lives to be reformed by this call to servanthood while holding steadfast to our dominating structures and organizational models.

The truth is that current models of church organization are not set up to support members engaging in mission and ministry but to support the clearinghouse function of leadership. If the current structures *serve* anyone, it is the leaders. To a great extent, the way that these structures serve leaders is by reinforcing the idea that they are to function as gatekeepers or a clearinghouse.

I know several pastors who are fortunate to actually have parishioners who want to engage in mission and ministry, but, because of the structures in place, the majority of the pastors' work with these people involves helping them navigate the labyrinthine rules and procedures that might otherwise impede them. There's a reason people see the various steps in the process as hoops to be jumped through—that is exactly what they are. In practice, all the process boils down to is extended vetting. "If you cannot complete these steps and clear these hurdles, then you probably shouldn't be engaging in the mission of God anyhow. Who do you think you are, thank you very much! We need you to prove to us that you are worthy of attaching the name of First Church to whatever you're doing. We will not have you embarrassing us."

Is it any wonder that people are leaving our churches? It has precious little to do with being conservative or liberal. It has to do with a dominant image of a God who operates through command and control rather than empowering and enabling.

Leaders Lead

In his book *Strengths Based Leadership*, author Tom Rath offers a profound insight: "You are a leader only if others follow." Leaders have followers—people who go with them on a journey of importance. If no one goes with you, you cannot be called a leader. He continues,

> Yet, we continue to focus on leaders and all but ignore their impact on, and the opinion of, the people they lead.

One problem is that we have studied leaders in isolation from the connections that make them great. As legendary investor Warren Buffett puts it, by definition, "A leader is someone who can get things done *through* other people." So while a leader's opinions may be interesting to study, that might not be the right unit of measurement for understanding why a person follows one leader and ignores another.[4]

What Rath and Buffett offer us are two fruitful areas of inquiry: why people follow a leader, and what it is that a leader "gets done *through* other people."

From 2005 to 2008, Gallup formally studied this question of why people follow certain leaders. Through their exhaustive study, they discovered that people follow a leader because they possess four characteristics: trust, compassion, stability, and hope.[5]

In their study, Gallup found that *trust* was the most important characteristic a leader could possess. Does this person do what she says she is going to do? Other words cited in the Gallup study were *honesty, integrity*, and *respect*. Trust is the grease that gets the wheels of partnership and collaboration going.

In pressing further, Gallup discovered that the way in which trust is communicated is by building relationships with people. According to Rath, observation teams relayed that successful teams talked very little about trust; it was simply present. Concurrent with the argument of this book, Rath notes, "Relationship flat-out trumps competence in building trust."[6]

Do you, as a leader, spend valuable time building relationships with those you are called to lead?

Compassion is the second characteristic of leaders people will follow. Do leaders really care about those they are called to lead? Is it clear, in everything they are doing, that the well-being of others is the most important consideration? Rath notes that people who experience love and care are more likely to stay with an organization and are more likely to engage the mission of the organization. This can be a word of hope for churches that consider themselves to be small: because of your size, you can outcare anyone. Small churches are small enough that everyone can be known and loved, so lean into that strength in a big way.

The third characteristic the Gallup research cites is *stability*. The entire premise of this book is built on the fact that changes are afoot and they are worrisome to our congregations. In these times, people want leaders who are stable to guide them. They want to know that the people they have called to be their servant-leaders are people who are not shaken. Part of this involves knowing that our leaders have good priorities. They know what is important and what is not. They are people who have the ability to be proactive, not reactive. The actions of reactive people are tied to whatever is happening. Proactive people may respond to current events, but their actions are informed by something much deeper and more solid.

The writer of Proverbs reminds us, "Where there is no vision the people perish" (Prov. 29:18). If a people are going to survive, then they need to see a vision of where they can go. Possessing *hope* is the fourth characteristic of leaders people will follow. Interestingly, providing people with a hopeful future—offering them guidance and direction—is the best way to provide a sense of stability.

Leaders: The Linchpin of an Organization

But if Warren Buffett's claim is that a leader gets things done through others, what is the leader's product? What is it that gets done?

The previous chapter ended with the question, how do churches coordinate various decentralized ministry and mission groups if we do not use command and control? Jesus would have us to be leaders, but our method of leadership must not be command and control. Ours must be a leadership of service. The way to coordinate the various groups has to be based on enabling and empowering them, not controlling them. How does that happen?

Leaders at all levels of the church serve their people when they fulfill three essential functions: proclaimers, facilitators, and mentors.

PROCLAIMERS

Every day we see it. As we move through our lives, millions of people manage to get from here to there with a measure of relative ease. Sure, accidents happen, but if you were able to take a step back and observe the movements of humanity, you would notice a flow, a rhythm, an order among the chaos.

These big coordinated movements depend on smaller actions working in synchronicity. In the United States, when things are flowing this smoothly, it is because people are generally walking on the right side of the sidewalk. Sure, not everyone does it (perhaps you don't always do it), but people in this country have an understanding, so deeply ingrained in most of us, that all of our coordinated movement as a people is tied to it. When we learn how to drive and the instructor tells us to drive on the right side of the road, we chuckle because we know that already. In fact, we have known to move on the right side since we were in preschool when our class took its first trip to the bathroom. We might even laugh at those parts of the world and their crazy penchant for driving on the left. What kind of person drives on the left? A crazy person. That, or a person who is trying to cause a wreck!

In *The Wisdom of Crowds* James Surowiecki tells of a man named Thomas C. Schelling, a social scientist. One day he asked a group of students, if they were going to meet someone in New York City but they didn't know where and had no way of talking to them beforehand, where they would go. New York, of course, is a big place; yet a majority of people who answered the question said the same thing: They would go to the information booth at Grand Central Station. Schelling complicated the problem a bit and told them they didn't know *when* they were supposed to meet their friend. Again, out of all the times during the day, the majority of people said they would arrive at noon.[7]

Schelling suggested that there are focal points upon which a majority of us will converge—conceptual landmarks that serve as guides for us. What have become known as "Schelling points" make a couple of things clear to us. First, we can move through life in some semblance of coordination when we intend to. It is a rarity to find a person who loves chaos. Most of us prefer some form of order in varying degrees. Second, our understandings of the world are surprisingly similar to others. The reason Schelling's students all picked noon at Grand Central Station as the time and place to arrive is that those ideas have cultural relevance. Sure, people from other places have different conceptual landmarks, but the fact remains that we truly live quite similar lives.

Further, Schelling understood that one did not have to wait for these landmarks to appear. A person could help that process along. He was teaching a class on an upper floor of a building. The stairwells were very narrow and often jammed with people trying to go up and down. It was a pain. Schelling got an idea.

One day he enlisted the help of one of his classes, asking them to begin using one of the stairwells to go up and a different one to go down. After three days, the ways students moved up and down the stairs in the building changed—all with no one giving explicit instructions except those Schelling gave to one class of students. Just like walking on the right, the new pattern for moving between floors in this building became habit. I'm sure that students today still move the same way in Schelling's old building, and I'm sure that the rogue student gets dirty looks for not adhering to "the rules."

What Schelling did was set a norm. He didn't have to beat people into submission. He simply enlisted the help of a small group of people to set a pattern. Remember social proofing? When a small but significant group of people starts communicating the message, "This is how we behave. This is how we approach things," it takes root.

The first job of congregational leaders is to proclaim the norms and expectations of the community—the parameters within which the community functions and the hopeful vision of where God is calling us. And leaders need to do this in such a way that it can become internalized in the lives of congregation members.

Remember the discussion about knowing the difference between big things and little things? Proclaiming norms, patterns, and expectations is a big thing. Frankly, almost anyone can figure out how to coordinate a fall clean-up day around the church or organize vacation Bible school or make sure there are ushers on Sunday mornings. But the call of the congregational leaders is to discern and communicate—to proclaim—the broad norms, parameters, and expectations that God has set for the community. This is a big thing, and we know that our leaders will do this job well, because we already know that groups excel when it comes to important decisions.

Just as *Wikipedia* answered the question, What is our purpose? with "To be an encyclopedia and ensure that everyone has access to the sum of all human knowledge," church boards need to ask the question, What is the purpose of the congregation, specifically our congregation? What is this congregation's DNA? Why did God gather this group of people in this place? How does peace and justice need to be realized here? The answer might change from time to time (hopefully not too often), but there is no other way for a congregation to know what norms, parameters, and expectations God expects them to operate in right now if their leaders do not discern them and communicate them clearly.

Congregational leaders also need to establish a set of *behavioral* norms. In the congregation I serve, we have a few phrases we use often—"Big kids take care of the little kids," "No is a good answer," "We don't choose God, God chooses us." All of us understand that our jobs are to care for those who cannot and will not care for themselves, that we don't have to be guilted into doing anything, and that our position before God is one of humility. These behavioral understandings shape our interactions with one another. If we know that we are a "big kid" in some way, we look for ways to take care of those who need our resources. This might mean we regularly volunteer in the nursery or engage in missional activity.

Leaders can ensure these norms, patterns, and expectations become internalized by consistently communicating them to the groups they serve. Those who preach and teach have a particularly special opportunity to proclaim them.

Every Sunday of the year, I get a chance to remind the group of people I serve what our values are. Every week, when I look at the Scripture passages, I try to find a way to tie the main point back to our norms, patterns, and expectations. If a passage suggests the topic of immigration, I try to get to (as pastor and author Rob Bell puts it) "the thing behind the thing" and look at the ways God would have us care for the "aliens and strangers" in our midst. By equating care for aliens and strangers with being "big kids who care for little kids," I am helping proclaim the norms, patterns, and expectations of our community while allowing people the freedom to live those norms in various ways.

Rather than attempt to tell people what to do in specific situations, congregational leaders should focus their energies on establishing communitywide norms and values that will, frankly, infect the lives of those in our congregations. Every week in worship, the congregation I serve sings a song called "All Are Welcome" by church musician Marty Haugen. Adding this easy little tune was a simple change to our service, but I did so because I wanted people to internalize a sense of inclusiveness. How can we sing "All Are Welcome" week after week and then try to exclude people? I don't have to tell people to be welcoming and inclusive; they sing it to themselves every week (and it helps that it's a great song!).

What are the big questions your congregation, regional body, or denomination needs to answer? What are the values (norms, patterns, and expectations) you need to establish? What is the purpose of your particular group? If you can answer those questions and figure out how to communicate those answers simply and clearly (catch phrases are great), you are well on your way to fulfilling the first function of a congregational leader.

FACILITATORS

While it is true that the most amazing ideas can come from a wide variety of places, it is also true that not everyone is skilled at participating in a meeting. Being a good group participant is, as my elementary and preschool age children will tell you, something that people need to work on.

I remember once when my oldest son came home from kindergarten and told us that on that day they had learned about ignoring people. What? That seemed to be the epitome of rudeness. Why would his teacher give him a lesson in that? Because, he explained, sometimes there were people in a group who could not stop talking. If he was going to complete his work, he was going to have to learn to ignore those people so that he could concentrate.

What I still find amazing as I recall that little scene is how gifted my son's teacher was. She had been in the game for better

than three decades and was exactly the kind of teacher my wife
and I had hoped for. Under all her soft and gentle ways, she was
serious business. When kids misbehaved, she was compassionate
enough to recognize what their domestic life was probably like
and she used that recognition to find a solution to the problem.
However, she was also tough enough to remind kids, "Good behavior is always the expectation." She wanted kids to learn how
to effectively communicate with one another, but she was wise
enough to know that is not always possible. And so sometimes
the best gift you can give kids when teaching them about communication is how to ignore someone who won't stop talking.

As I touched on in chapters 3 and 4, when a group of diverse
people is gathered, they are naturally going to have many different experiences and understandings about what is happening
and what needs to be done. There will be a lot of opinions and
ideas. There will be different kinds of personalities. *Someone* has
to manage that.

The second job of congregational leaders is that of group
facilitator. Navigating a group of people through a process is a
learned skill. It takes only a little bit of training before someone
can read the temperature in a room and decide whether the heat
needs to be turned up or whether the boiling pot needs to be
taken off the stove for a while. One *can* learn to watch the body
language of people in a room and figure out who is frustrated
because they have not had an opportunity to speak. It does
not take much training to learn effective ways of cutting in on
someone when they have begun speaking for the twelfth time
on that particular topic.

In many cases, a group's problems can be solved by setting
expectations at the beginning of its time together. Establishing
the method of discussion beforehand is key to making sure
that a group functions properly. If everyone knows there will
be a time when each person will be able to share or reflect, the

chances of a heated exchange while trying to make a point will be significantly less.

Regardless, congregational leaders must learn to facilitate the group process well so that all the private information that makes a group wise can surface. These are skills that pastors are (or should be) taught in their training. Pastors should pay that favor forward and teach the other leaders they work with.

MENTORS

Proclamation and facilitation generally occur within the context of a group, but the third job of the congregational leader occurs primarily with an eye toward the individual. As stated in the Warren Buffett quote earlier, "A leader is someone who can get things done *through* other people." The way that this most effectively happens is when a leader uses her gifts, skills, and passions to draw out, connect, and amplify the gifts, skills, and passions of congregation members. Being a mentor to others can occur in a variety of ways: by naming a calling, by helping people discover a calling, and by protecting the process.

Naming a calling is one way to be a mentor. Helping people find where they fit is an important job. Every year as we begin our search for new elders and deacons, I say to the nominating committee, "Sometimes our job is to help them see in themselves what everyone else sees in them." But just because you say, "You are called!" doesn't mean they will believe it; they need opportunities to find these things in themselves. Congregational leaders need to provide regular opportunities for members to discover things about themselves they never knew.

One summer a couple of years ago, I met with twelve people and engaged them in a multiweek process by which they discovered their gifts, skills, and passions. Out of that group came three deacons, three elders, and four others who started a large-scale ongoing mission project we have been involved in ever since. What had been holding them back? A lack of knowledge of who they were.

Helping people discover a calling is another way to be a mentor. Many people have been touched by the proclamation of the Word and feel a fire in their belly. But many of them have never felt that fire before or have ignored it when they have. What do they do about that fire? Where do they go? How do they work to address the burning passion inside of them? Congregational leaders should see it as their jobs to connect people to various needs in the world.

As a part of the multiweek discovery process, the cofacilitators and I arranged for ten local social service organizations to talk to the group. They spent time describing what they do and why they do it and answering any questions the group had. Several people told me afterwards, "That was great. I don't feel called to any of those things, but at least I can cross them off my list and keep looking." Sometime the best thing leaders can do is connect the right people with the right project.

Protecting the process is a third way to mentor. Unlike command-and-control leaders, mentoring leaders see their job not as controlling content but as protecting process. Along with helping people see their potential and helping them discover needs that can be addressed, leaders should also make sure members know the steps they need to take to begin a mission or ministry project in their congregation. They need to be told that there will be no roadblocks. They need to know that they will not have to endure painful committee meetings only to have their requests denied. As long as the mission or ministry project they want to pursue fits with the congregation's norms, patterns, and expectations, they need to know they will be supported with resources and advice.

A Return to Gratis and *Libre*

So, what is it that a leader *gets done* through others? Ultimately, it is mission and ministry, but the leaders of an open source church will understand that the best way to ensure these things happen is by opening up the process to the entire congregation. In truth, the model of leadership an open source church supposes circles around to the place where this book started: *gratis* and *libre*. While leaders are libre, subject to none and free to call the congregation to places it cannot yet imagine, they are also gratis, called to give up their power to become servants of the whole church.

It is this openness that is the true ministry of the leader, for openness is needed not only in the church but also in the entire world in which we live. By modeling openness to their congregation, leaders demonstrate that openness is a viable option for engaging with others. By respecting the freedoms of their congregation, they encourage them to respect the freedoms of others.

~ Conclusion ~

A New Thing

I am an ordained member of the Presbyterian Church (USA), a denomination that has participated in significant ways in proclaiming the gospel of Jesus Christ in the past two hundred years, not only in the United States but also abroad. The institutional habits of our church have been long established and have served us well. I assume you can say the same thing about your religious tradition. Mine is not the only church to have borne witness to God's work in the world, nor is it the only one to affect the lives of the various communities in which the church is present. But here we are, well into a new millennium, and our various churches are being called into something new and fresh, something we have not previously encountered, but something exciting nonetheless.

And lest we become afraid of this new thing, we should remind ourselves that God is guiding us now, just as God has always been the one guiding us.

"Pray to the LORD on Its Behalf"

The prophet Jeremiah was making everyone mad. In the war of the ancient superpowers, the little kingdom of Judah had fallen prey to Babylon, and God's people were about to be sent into exile. That they were anxious about what this meant for them as a people and for their future is understandable.

Other than Jeremiah, every prophet in the land was trying to make the best of the situation by telling the people that they would have to endure exile for only two years before they would be on their way back home to resume life as normal. After two years, these prophets said, God would break the power of the Babylonians and Judah would be restored.

But Jeremiah knew it wasn't going to be that easy. He knew that the cheap hope the other prophets were offering was exactly that—cheap hope—because God intended for the people to be in exile for seventy years. Their only hope was to adjust their perspective on the situation—to see it in a new light, to see it for what it really was. If Jeremiah could get them to see what was really in front of them, exile might become more than an experience they had to survive. It would become a place in which they could thrive.

On the advent of their departure, Jeremiah spoke these words from God: "Build houses and live in them; plant gardens and eat what they produce. Take wives and have sons and daughters; take wives for your sons, and give your daughters in marriage, that they may bear sons and daughters; multiply there, and do not decrease. But seek the welfare of the city where I have sent you into exile, and pray to the LORD on its behalf, for in its welfare you will find your welfare" (Jer. 29:5–7). Other than the sage advice to give themselves fully to their new home ("build houses, . . . plant gardens"), the key to this passage is the call to pray for "the city where I have sent you."

In Jewish tradition, acts of prayer and supplication to God occurred at the temple. When one wanted to petition God, that petition was made at the temple and accompanied by a sacrifice. Now the people were being told that while they were in Babylon, they were to pray for their new home. But where, exactly, were they supposed to do that?

This was a fundamental shift in the people's understanding of their relationship to God. God was no longer limited to the temple in Jerusalem. They now understood that God was everywhere. Their religious practices and therefore their religion had to be modified if it was to continue to offer the freedom that it had always promised. I think it is safe to say that if their religion had not changed, it would have died.

New Ways

As God's people, we have always had to conceive of new ways to respond to God's call to mission and ministry. Countless models and understandings of God and God's call to the church have emerged over the centuries, and there will, no doubt, be countless more. As I have said repeatedly throughout this book, churches everywhere are encountering a shift in cultural expectations, the likes of which (according to Phyllis Tickle in her book *The Great Emergence*) the world has not seen in five hundred years. It seems that everything is different, even from just fifty short years ago.

We can learn a lesson from the exiled Hebrew people: when we enter a new time and a new place, we must change the way we do business if we are to survive. We can be certain that the change will be difficult, and that there will be many hard conversations and even arguments. But if the exiled Hebrews can figure out how to pray in Babylon without their temple, surely we can be faithful enough to heed God's call and attend to mission and ministry in our day and age.

Notes

CHAPTER ONE: THE OPEN SOURCE CHURCH

1. Bruce Perens, "The Open Source Definition," Open Sources: Voices from the Open Source Revolution, January 1999, http://oreilly.com/catalog/opensources/book/perens.html.
2. "The Open Source Definition (Annotated)," version 1.9, Open Source Initiative, http://www.opensource.org/osd.html.
3. James Cone, *Black Theology and Black Power* (Maryknoll, NY: Orbis Books, 1997), 34.
4. Jerome Berryman, *The Complete Guide to Godly Play* (New York: Church Publishing, 2002), 79.
5. David Flanagan, "Java Examples in a Nutshell," 1997, O'Reilly.com, http://examples.oreilly.com/jenut/Portfolio.java.
6. Perens, "Open Source Definition."
7. "Open Source Definition (Annotated)."
8. Ibid.

CHAPTER TWO: CHURCH AS WIKIPEDIA

1. "History of Wikipedia," *Wikipedia*, http://en.wikipedia.org/wiki/History_of_Wikipedia#Formulation_of_the_concept.
2. "Wikipedia: What Wikipedia Is Not," *Wikipedia*, http://en.wikipedia.org/wiki/Wikipedia:What_Wikipedia_is_not.
3. Ibid.
4. "Wikipedia: Five Pillars," *Wikipedia*, http://en.wikipedia.org/wiki/Wikipedia:Five_pillars.

5. A TED (for technology, entertainment, and design) conference is an invitation-only conference that gathers the world's brightest minds and gives each person eighteen minutes to enlighten the crowd about "ideas worth spreading."
6. *Book of Order, The Constitution of the Presbyterian Church (U.S.A.), Part 2* (Louisville, KY: Presbyterian Church [USA], 2009), G-1.0200.
7. "Wikipedia: Five Pillars."
8. "GCR 2.3—Not Your Mama's Church: Women, Creativity, and Emergence," GodComplexRadio.com, http://godcomplexradio.com/2010/05/gcr-2-3-not-your-mamas-church-women-creativity-emergence/.
9. "Wikipedia: Five Pillars."
10. Jack Haberer, *Godviews: The Convictions That Drive Us and Divide Us* (Louisville, KY: Westminster John Knox, 2001).
11. "Wikipedia: Five Pillars."
12. Ibid.
13. "The Birth of Wikipedia: Jimmy Wales on TED.com," TED Blog, http://blog.ted.com/2009/08/10/The_birth_of_wi/.
14. James Surowiecki, *The Wisdom of Crowds* (New York: Anchor Books, 2004), 3.
15. Ibid., 4.
16. Ibid., 22.

CHAPTER THREE: YOUR FRIENDLY NEIGHBORHOOD CHURCH EXPERT

1. "Raising Up Leaders for the Mission of God: A Report of the Presbyterian Church (USA) Joint Committee on Leadership Needs" (February 2010), 3.
2. James Surowiecki, *The Wisdom of Crowds* (New York: Anchor Books, 2004), 32.
3. *Journal of Personality and Social Psychology* 77, no. 6, 1121–34, http://www.scirp.org/journal/psych (December 2009).
4. Ibid.
5. Surowiecki, *Wisdom of Crowds*, xv.
6. Malcolm Gladwell, "None of the Above," *New Yorker*, December 17, 2007, http://newyorker.com/arts/critics/books/2007/12/17/071217crbo_books_gladwell.
7. Ibid.
8. *Book of Order: The Constitution of the Presbyterian Church (U.S.A.), Part 2* (Louisville, KY: Presbyterian Church [USA], 2009), G-6.0106.

9. "Groupthink," *Wikipedia*, http://en.wikipedia.org/wiki/ Groupthink.

CHAPTER FOUR: SO IF EVERYONE ELSE JUMPED OFF THE BRIDGE, WOULD YOU?

1. "Episode 5—Nadia Bolz-Weber," Godcomplexradio.com, http://god-complexradio.com/2009/05/episode-5-nadia-bolz-weber/.
2. Nadia Bolz-Weber, *Salvation on the Small Screen: 24 Hours of Christian Television* (New York: Church Publishing, 2008), 107.
3. James Surowiecki, *The Wisdom of Crowds* (New York: Anchor Books, 2004), 43.
4. Ibid., 41.
5. Ibid., 55.
6. Ibid., xv.
7. Ibid., 49.
8. Ibid., 64.

CHAPTER FIVE: LETTING GO, OR THE ART OF DECENTRALIZATION

1. Paul Vitello, "Taking a Break from the Lord's Work," *New York Times* (August 1, 2010), http://www.nytimes.com/2010/08/02/ nyregion/02burnout.html.
2. Based on an illustration by Bill Easum, from his video, "The Top-Down, Command-and-Control, Stifling Story," *Unfreezing Moves* (Port Aransas, TX: 21st Century Strategies, 2006), videocassette.
3. James Surowiecki, *The Wisdom of Crowds* (New York: Anchor Books, 2004), 70–71.
4. Ibid., 71.

CHAPTER SIX: LEADERS LEAD, BUT EXPERTS DO WHAT, EXACTLY?

1. William Loader, "Pentecost 20," First Thoughts on Year B Gospel Passages from the Lectionary, author's webpage, http://wwwstaff.murdoch. edu.au/~loader/MkPentecost20.htm.
2. Brian A. Wren, *Praying Twice: The Music and Words of Congregational Song* (Louisville, KY: Westminster John Knox, 2000), 230.
3. *Book of Order: The Constitution of the Presbyterian Church (U.S.A.), Part 2* (Louisville, KY: Presbyterian Church [USA], 2009), ch. 3.
4. *Strengths Based Leadership* (Washington, DC: Gallup Press, 2009), 79.

5. Ibid., 82–91.
6. Ibid., 85.
7. James Surowiecki, *The Wisdom of Crowds* (New York: Anchor Books, 2004), 90–91.